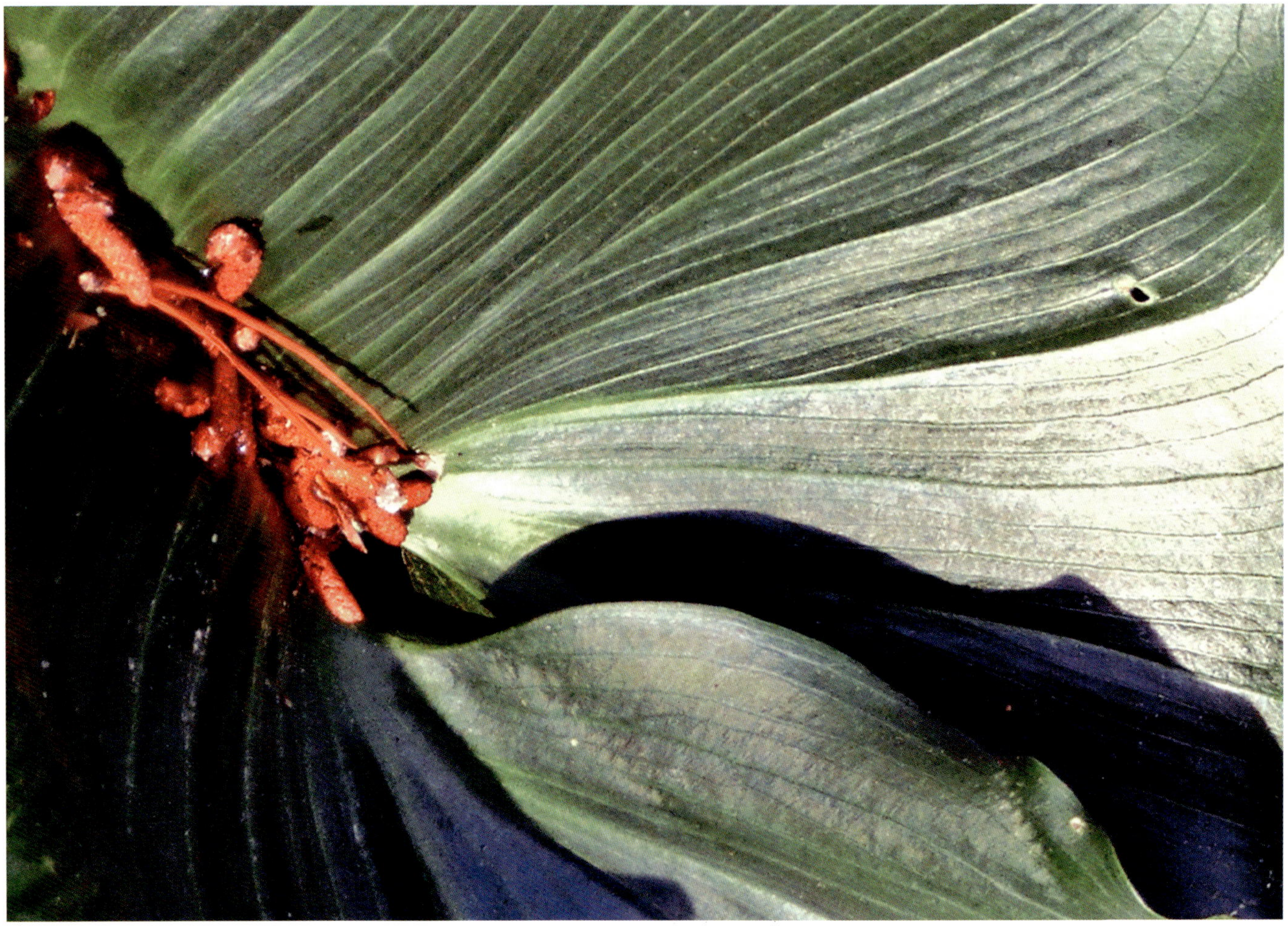

STONE MUSIC

The Art and Poetry of Susan Gardner

Red Mountain Press

For Katarina —

Susan Gardner

18 June 2023

Design by Michael Motley

Printed in Canada by Friesens

Cover and Frontispiece:
Composition with Red, Rochefort
2007, Photograph, 5 x 7 inches

Half Title: *La Altura detail*
1984, Oil on canvas, 28 x 20 inches

Right: *Kew Palm, London*
2001, Photograph, 5 x 7 inches

RED MOUNTAIN PRESS
P.O. Box 32205
Santa Fe, New Mexico 87594
redmountainpress.us

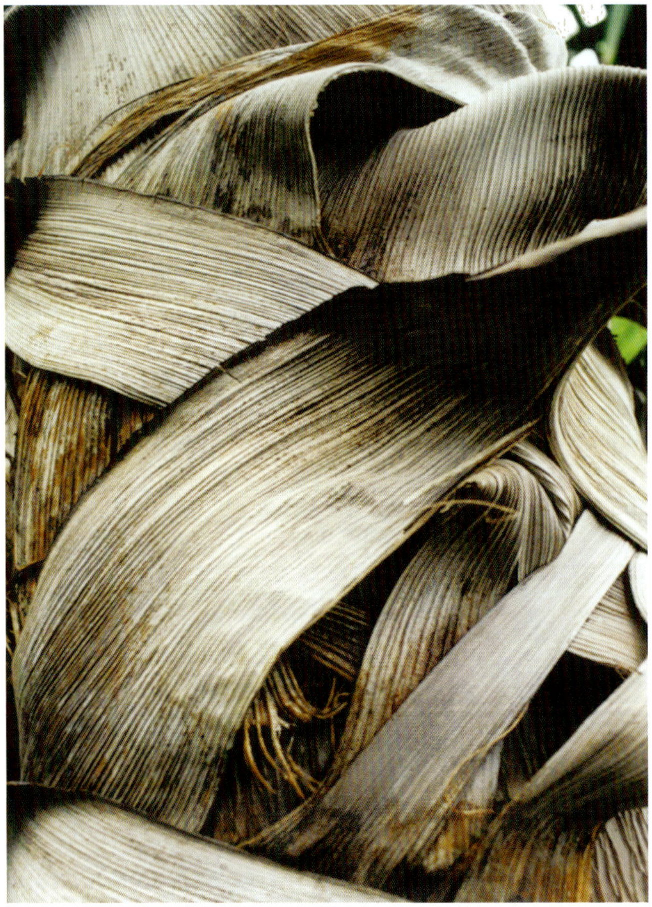

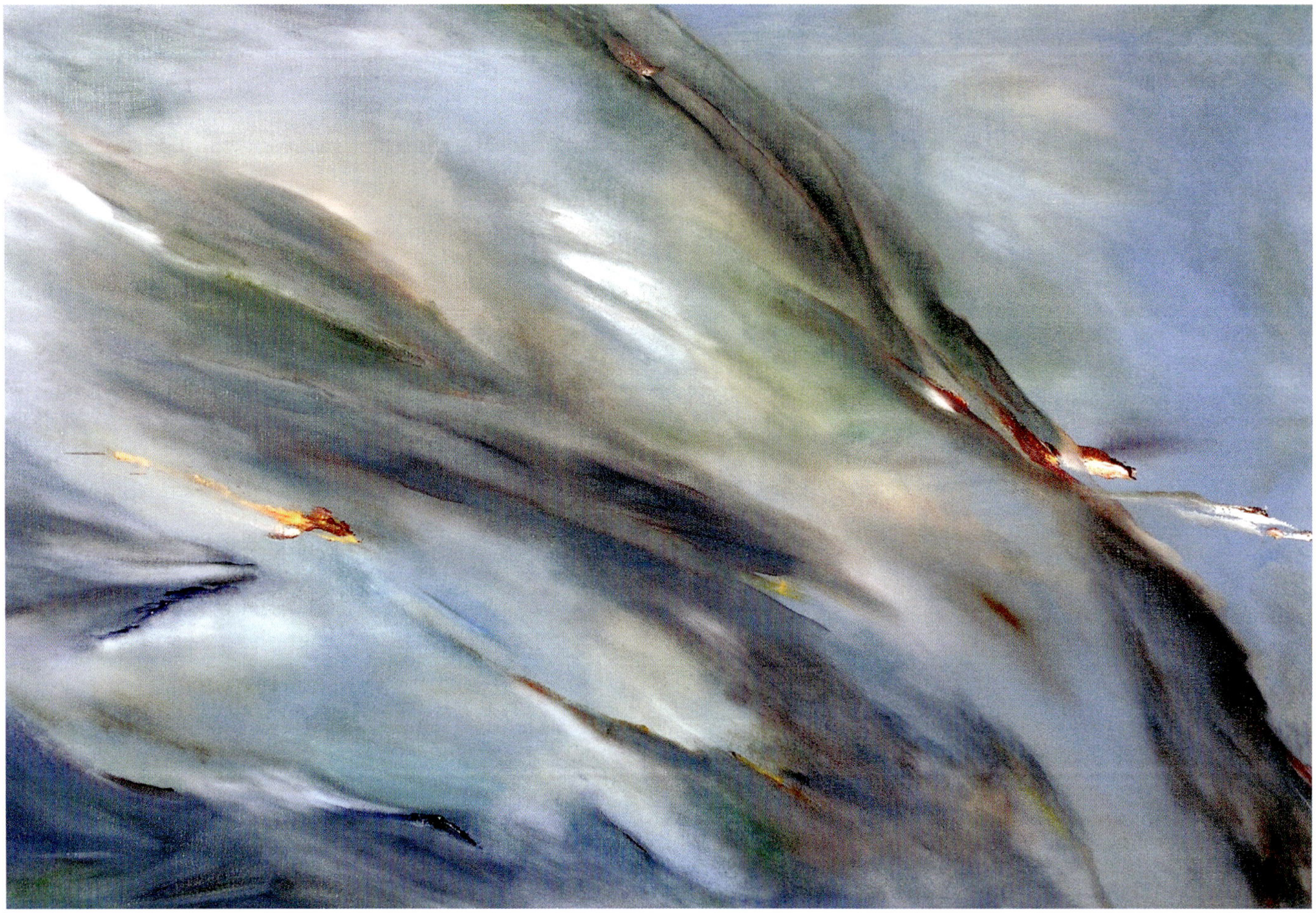

For RDR

PREFACE

Making art appears to be a solitary activity with long hours in the studio, the artist alone with the muse. In fact, almost no one lives hermetically sealed off from the world. I would like to thank the Anderson Center for Interdisciplinary Studies, Red Wing, Minnesota; Can Serrat, Barcelona; and the government of Morbihan, France, which along with the Maryland Institute College of Art, invited me to the Chateau Rochefort. The generosity and encouragement of my fellow artists and the uninterrupted time are deeply felt and appreciated. Thanks to St. John's College, Santa Fe, for producing *Intimate Landscapes*. A few of these poems first appeared there in 1998 when the College hosted the exhibition of my photography from Korea.

Thanks to friends who patiently listened to and read the early drafts. You surely know who you are. I am grateful to Peter Michaelides for his insight and suggestions. Thanks to my son, Daniel Kern, who made many constructive observations.

My gratitude forever to RD, without whom this work would still be in the closet.

SG

East Wind 2004, Oil on linen, 46 x 32.5 inches

8

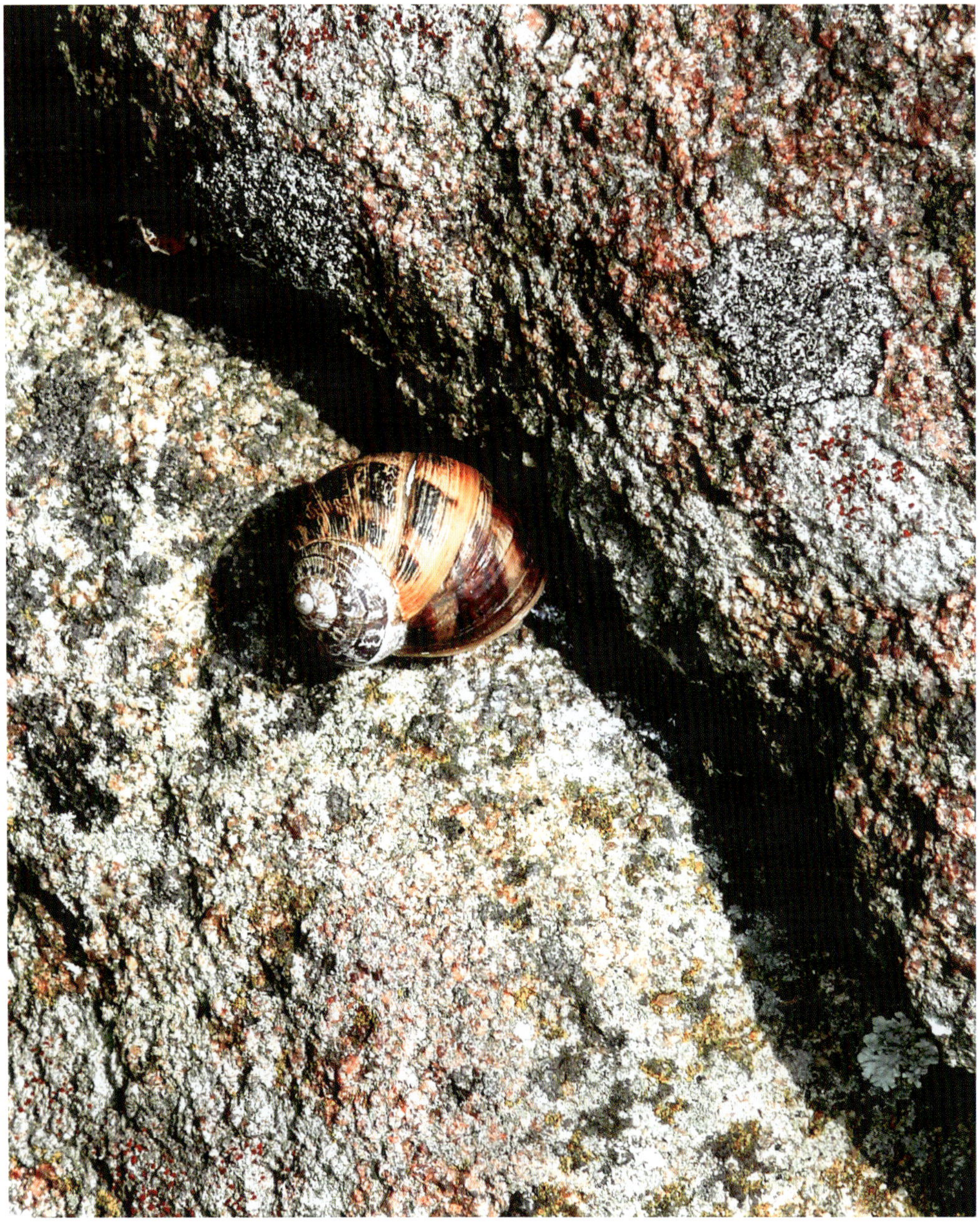

Snail on a Rock, Carnac 2007, Photograph, 8 x 10 inches

A WORD FROM THE ARTIST

My work begins in a silent uncluttered moment. I find a place to stand where I can aim for directness and transparency. I see the process being one of discovery — observing with open eyes the essential details of reality.

I explore the aesthetic connections we have with one another and with the natural environment. I try to describe the boundaries we maintain between ourselves, the ways that land becomes landscape due to our presence, and the ways we are all affected and resist being affected by our choices. Part of my job as an artist is to record, to make manifest what is true. My tools are brushes and paint, camera lens, pencil and words.

Painting begins in a field of physical perfection: the white paper or canvas surface, complete in itself, holds an infinity of possibilities. With the first stroke of my hand, this perfection is ruptured. It is a moment full of possibility, with the potential of encountering something worth the sacrifice of the perfect: the recognition of reality, a glimpse of beauty.

For me, painting is a total sensory and sensual experience: the texture of the materials, the sibilant sounds of the pencil and brushes as they cross the surface, the palette of colors, and the studio smells, heavy with associations of work. The pleasure of handling the tools is the physical essence of studio life. When all goes well, my brain remembers the delight of doing what I love best to do.

My poetry emerges in a similar process: in actively looking at the details of reality, observing aspects of nature and the human condition, giving the reader freedom and opportunity for active response. The work notes and sometimes comments on what is right in front of my face.

A few of the poems were originally composed in Japanese, either as calligraphy or as part of a painting. Several of the poems were originally in Spanish. In moving the work to English, I found that I couldn't translate the poems, but instead, recreated them. The differences in the music of these languages, the emphases and frameworks for forming the thought, were distinct enough that the poem became a new work, a cousin to the first.

Although usually made at separate times and places, my poetry, painting, and photography often consider similar ideas. They tread the boundary between representation and abstraction. I hope to find beauty in the rhythm and sound of words, the rhythm and line of visual imagery. In focusing on the presence of nature, I aim for delicacy and intensity, to say that nature exists as itself, and it is human perception that creates the sense and understanding of beauty.

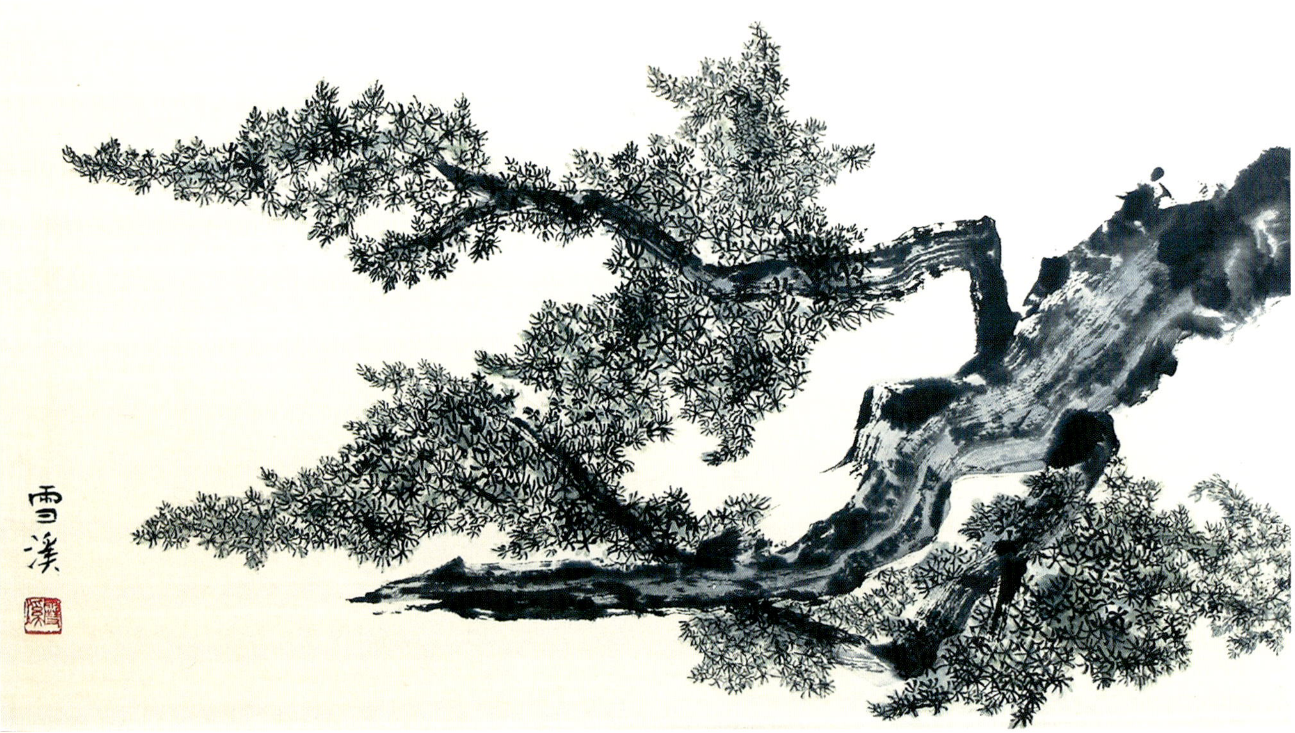

Pine Branch 1973, Sumi and Chinese inks on handmade Chinese paper, 18 x 38 inches
Shown at inaugural exhibition at the Main Gallery, Mitsui Bank, Kobe, Japan

ABOUT THE ARTIST

RD Ross

Susan Gardner is a uniquely accomplished artist with a consistent ability to extract contextual meaning from the subtle undertones of her surroundings and associations. Her work has grown and developed with each exploration of new situations, ideas, and cultures.

Beginning with Chinese landscape painting and calligraphy, and continuing through her expansive use of varied techniques, media, and visual experimentation, Gardner has always incorporated the essential qualities of her physical and personal surroundings. Her perceptions, as revealed in both visual and literary work, are at once focused, descriptive, and uncommon.

Gardner's childhood and college years were spent in New York City, where she enjoyed and later paticipated in that especially dynamic and varied arts milieu. The Museum of Modern Art became her teacher and refuge, a source of joy, amazement, and learning. She developed an open-ended appreciation for modern and contemporary artists who spoke thoughtfully and philosophically in visual language, who employed and sometimes discarded classical aesthetics in new and often startling ways.

In the 1960s, newly arrived in Korea, she studied and worked in classical Chinese landscape painting. Her master teacher, Park Se Won, gave her the painting name Sekkei, meaning *snow valley*. Traditionally, a painting name embodies an artist's character; *Sekkei* suggests the qualities of quiet solitude, self-directedness, and purity of thought. She lived in Japan for several years in the 1970s, developing technique and abilities in calligraphy and printmaking. She worked at the Atelier Petit and began to exhibit her work more widely. In 1976, she was invited to exhibit several of her prints in Tokyo, at the Japan National Association of University Women XXII Annual Invitational Print Exposition.

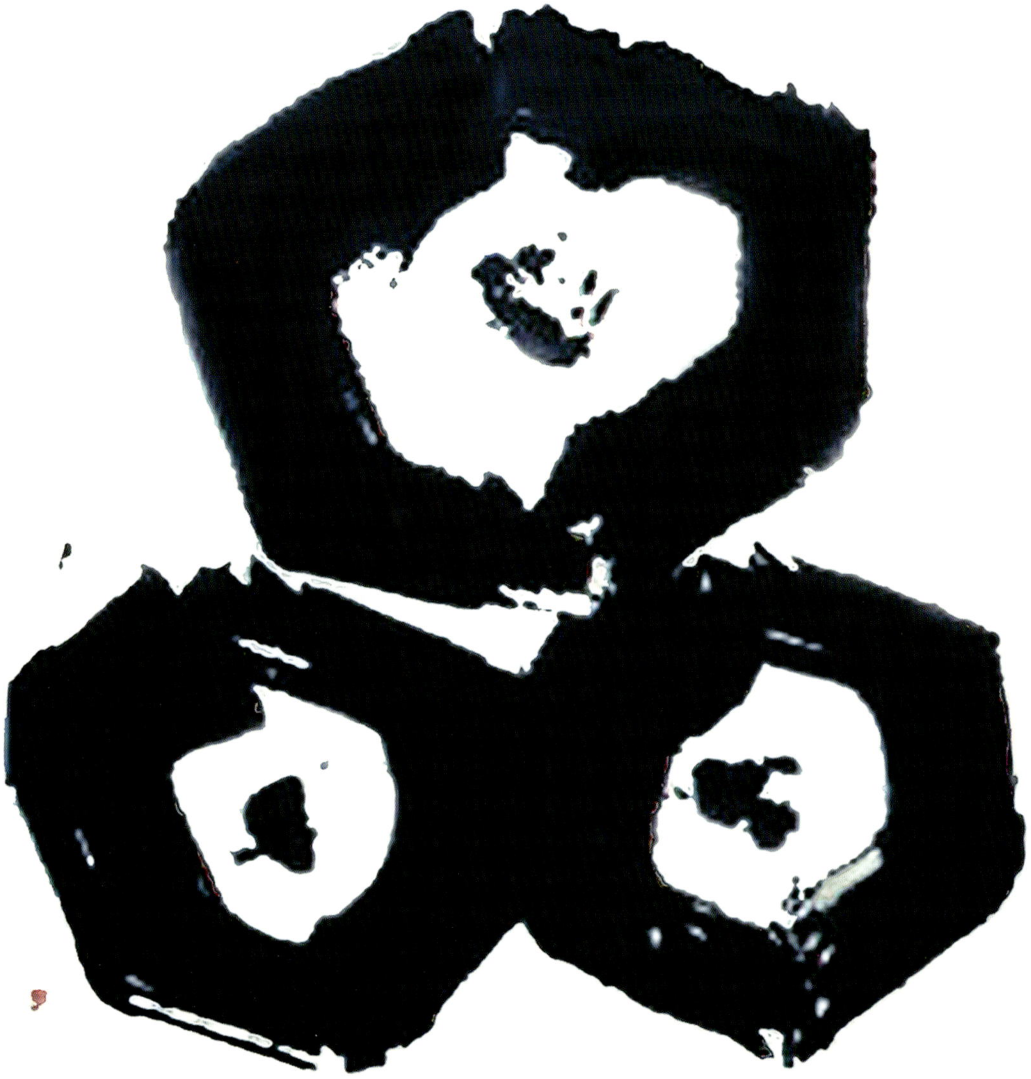

Hikari (Shining Light) 1975, Calligraphy, Sumi on handmade paper, 28 x 25 inches

Persimmon 1974, Lithograph, 16.5 x 18 inches (right)

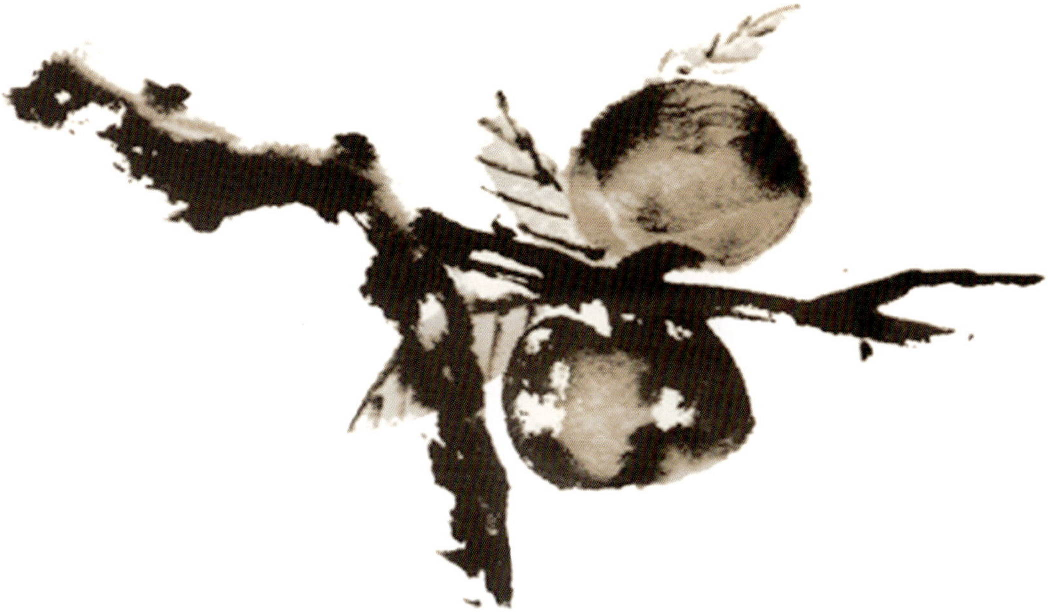

Gardner says that calligraphy opened her mind to ideas never before experienced. In calligraphy, with each character, the writer and reader encounter a whole, gestaltic idea, complete and indivisible. Gardner has taken this concept and applied it to her own work. By centering herself as she works, integrating mind and body, Gardner is able to achieve mastery of her chosen medium, creating an essential unity of content and materials. Given her inherent inclination toward direct, purposeful communication, Gardner displays in her work a vibrant sense of uncluttered, transparant clarity.

Many of the tools and attitudes Gardner now employs in her work reflect essential beliefs formed early in her development. One of these is the Buddhist concept of direct pointing: a person must intentionally move beyond the filter of personal ego to see the true nature of reality. Looking directly at the subject to find what is true in the here and now is a signature aspect of Gardner's visual and literary work.

These qualities are easily seen in her poetry, with its loose, conversational cadence and open, precise language. Rythmic and musical, Gardner's poems are often reminiscent of tanka and haiku in their subject matter and simplicity of imagery. Her photography and, to an even greater degree, her painting convey a similar lyrical rhythm, inviting the viewer to move into her world.

Over the course of 35 years Gardner has drawn subject matter and inspiration from the natural world in widely differing cultural settings. Her work has evolved through various choices of visual media, including oil painting, printmaking, ceramics, bronze sculpture, and mixed media.

Gardner's professional career began with several exhibitions in Japan during the 1970s. The first of these was installed at the Mitsui Bank main gallery, a prestigious venue in Kobe, and marked her initiation as a professional artist. She was the first foreign artist to be invited to join the Sei Boku Kai, a modernist calligraphy group in the Osaka-Kobe region. There were many more exhibitions in Kyoto, Osaka, and Tokyo, culminating with the Mikimoto Gallery in Tokyo.

In Mexico, she began for the first time to use traditional canvases with nontraditional media. *Manzanas de Amadeus* marked a turning point, pivotal for art and artist. In 1984, The Museum of Technology, in Mexico City, presented a retrospective of her work that then traveled to Guadalajara in 1985. The critic José Luis Meza Inda wrote in, *El Informador*:

> *[T]he the line of her drawings, as the execution of her landscapes ... [is] dynamic and vigorous, full of life and rhythm. They... recall in content and form a traditional significant simplicity of Kano and the motivating ideas of the Zen school, with their gestural searches, capable of synthesizing the aesthetic expression in a few marks of vigorous brushwork.*
>
> *Her landscapes, although much more elaborate than the drawings, seem in the same way uncomplicated and very elemental. ... It is necessary to keep in mind the great difficulty that is signified in reaching such a capacity for synthesis ....*
>
> *There are in those works a subtle and parsimonious use of color, reserved and discreet application of textures, and simplicity of drawing in the rhythmically placed orthographic chains; all of which gives, as a result, atmospheres full of suggestibility and intense lyricism.*

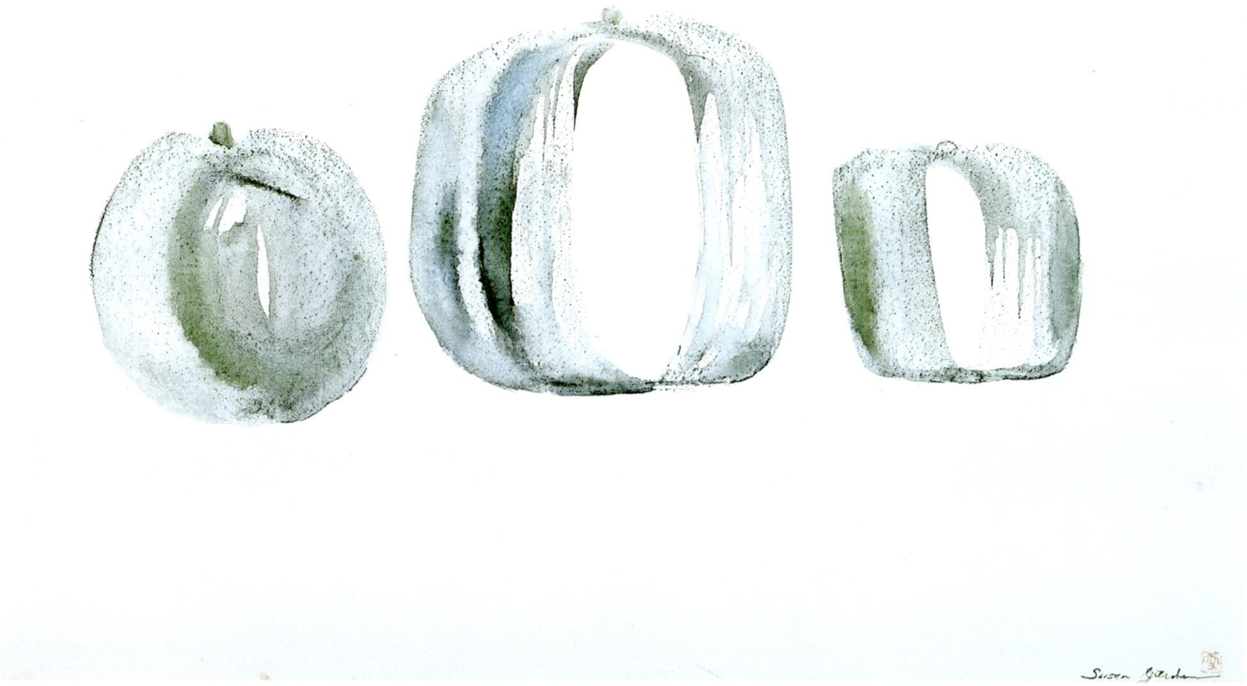

Manzanas de Amadeus 1982, Ink and pigments on canvas, 24 x 20 inches

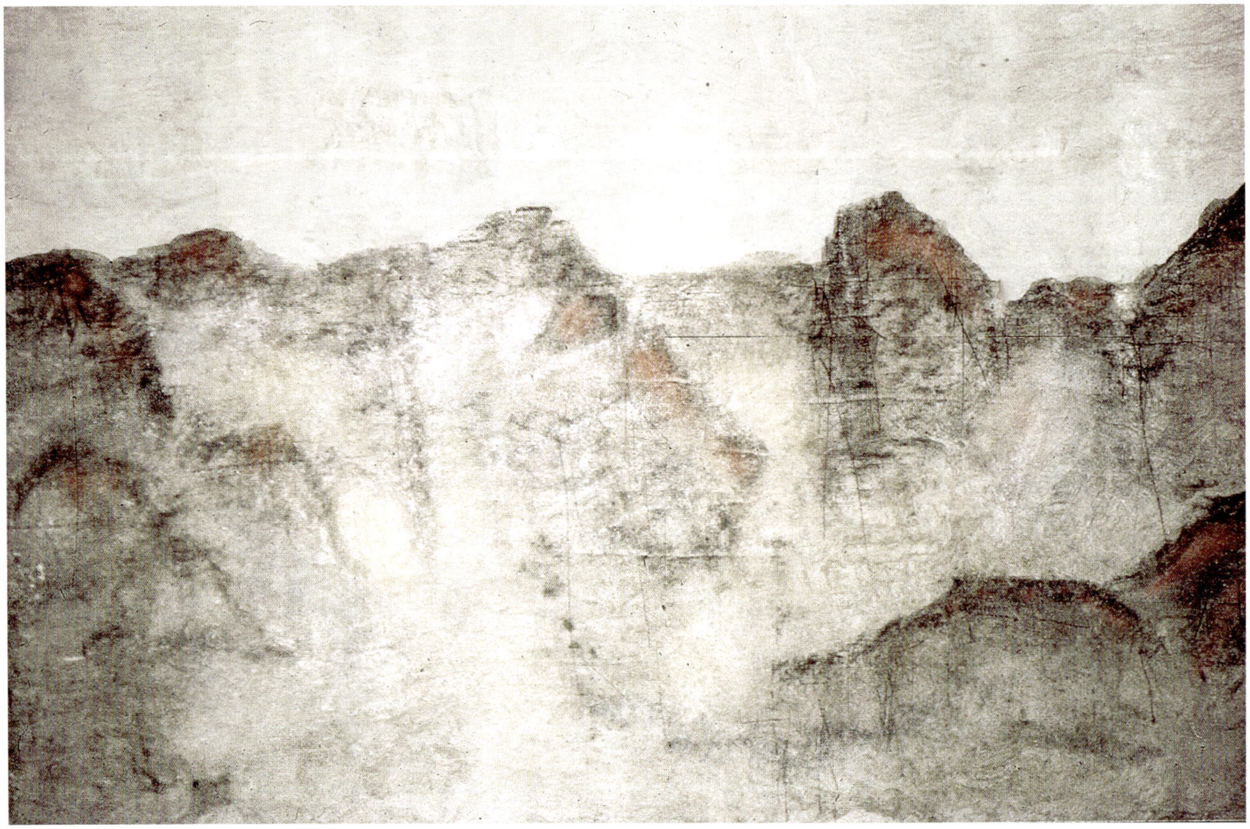

Red Mountain
1986, Mixed media on paper made by the artist
62 x 47 inches

Gardner believes that the essence of life's experiences will be evident in the work of any serious artist. Her years in Mexico during the 1980s were a time when new themes emerged and prompted experimentation with new materials. The Mexican environment provided the occasion for large-scale paper-making and ceramics and the evolving changes that followed in the painting. Her painting of 1986, *Red Mountain*, is an example. She says,

> *This is about seeing the color red. ... The lines that define the cliffs are calligraphy. Some are just lines, some are jokes to myself. There are ten word poems contained in this piece. I wanted to know something so well that I could paint its reality without having to be literally*

La Altura 1984, Inks and pigments on canvas, 28 x 20 inches *accurate. I wanted to cross between the literary and the visual. Craft elements confront each other and are joined in the piece.... Making art is a matter of trying to look around honestly, avoiding affectation. It is taking chances.*

J.W. Mahoney, the Washington, DC art critic, wrote in his critical catalogue essay in 1986:

It is in the western tradition to make distinctions between things and thoughts, between mind and nature, and, in its art, between object and ground, abstraction and figuration, fine art and craft. For a western artist coming to maturity in the east, as Susan Gardner has, such distinctions have become considerably less valid. What is most real is the process itself, guided by the greater conscious forces of nature; thus for the artist, the act of papermaking is an integral phase of the drama of her eventual image-making.

Susan Gardner's images ... arise as evenly, as naturally proper as the marks of high tide on a beach, as obviously and surprisingly as the geometric patterns of color on bird's wing. This is not mimesis, however, but synthesis, the conjunction of form and mood carried intuitively ... to the effortless purity of vision.

There is synthesis too, in her latticework of the acquired traditions — the great modernist masters — Matisse, Klee and Picasso — blend without a ripple into her training in Chinese landscape painting and Japanese calligraphy.

In a sense her work relates more to music: music alludes to the abstract flow that carries its rush of feelings ... through finite and infinite images. Susan Gardner is such a symbolist; her art speaks of what is not seen yet is present, of what is common and yet irredeemably precious.

While painting is always at the center of her work, Gardner continually explores new modes and media for recording and expressing her observations. In the 1990s, photography became a main component of her visual repertoire. Her first major exhibition of photography, *Intimate Landscapes*, was installed at St. John's College Gallery, Santa Fe, and was the occasion to

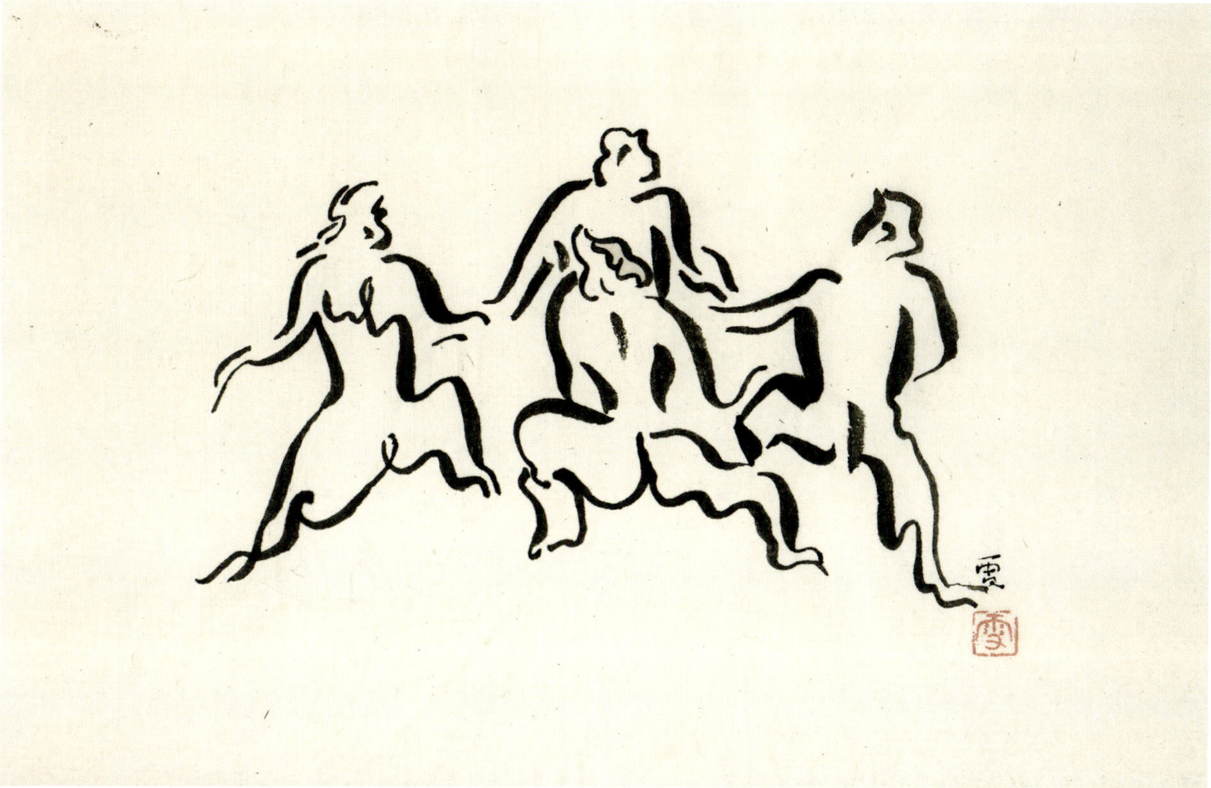

Dancers: Quartet
1984, Sumi on
handmade paper
9 x 12 inches

present her first published work of poetry, also titled *Intimate Landscapes*. Originally intended as wall text for the photographs, the poetry was produced by the College in a small edition.

Craig Smith wrote in the *Santa Fe New Mexican*, June 26, 1998, in an article titled "In the Land of Calm":

Behind the nearly 40 photographic images [in the exhibition] was Gardner's awareness of human interaction with history, tradition and the land. . . . [She] infuses her photography with an appreciation for line and a sense of stillness and simplicity.

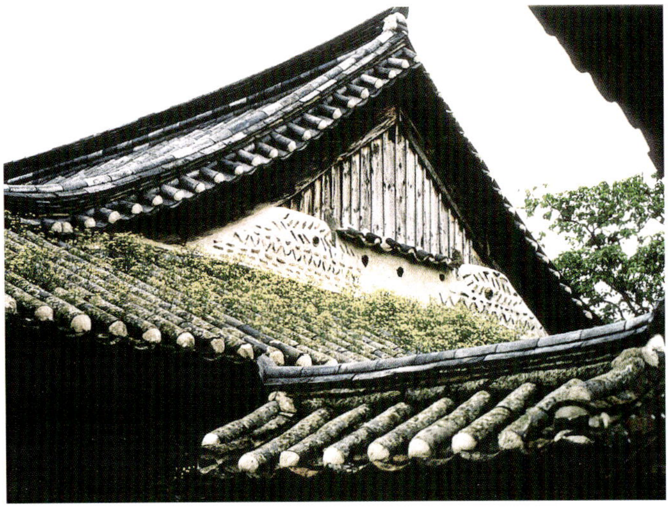

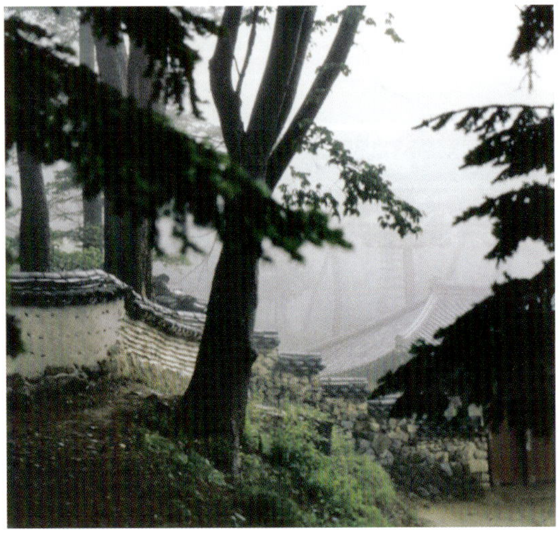

In addition to her photographic skill, Gardner is an established oil painter, ceramicist, paper expert, and calligrapher. So why did she choose to present her vision through the camera?

In her own words: [I]f I do calligraphy or paint in oil on canvas or use my camera ... I'm really thinking about the same thing. Each medium gives you a different mechanism ... [T]he camera is a more purely visual way of understanding and describing things.

Today Gardner works primarily as a painter, photographer, and poet. She continues to fill her art with a sense of lyrical spontaneity, of freshness in both form and content. As an artist at mid-career, she is fully mature in her understanding and execution. At the same time, and as a matter of personal choice, her development is thoroughly unfinished. Says Gardner, "The selection of form and materials, the act of exploring, and the process of taking risks are the basic tools of a human life, my life."

Boundary Wall, Heinsa 1987/1998, Photograph, 8 x 10 inches • *House of Yellow Flowers, Hahwae* 1987, Photograph, 8 x 10 inches

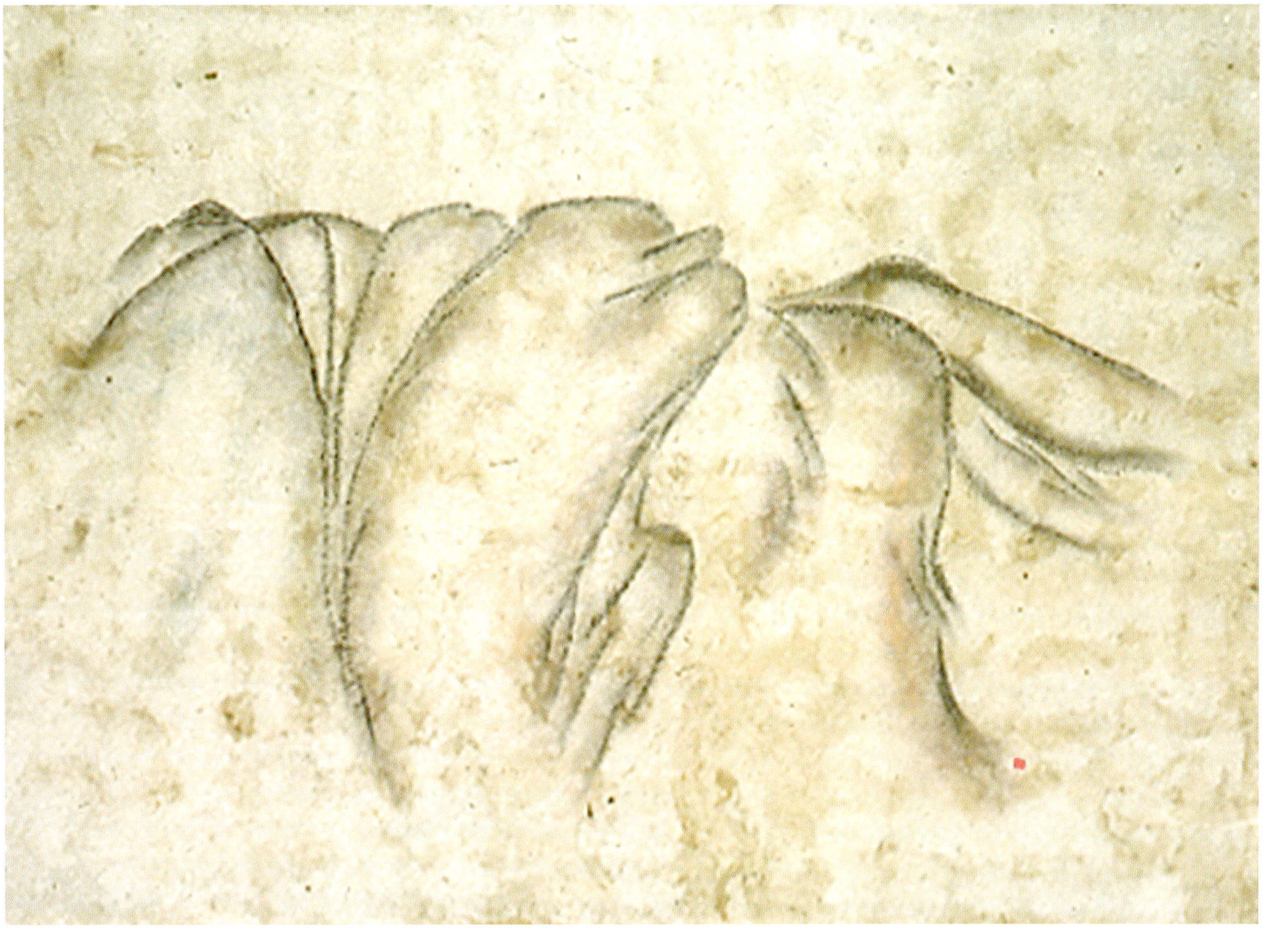

Al Borde 1984–85, Mixed media on paper made by the artist, 60 x 46 inches

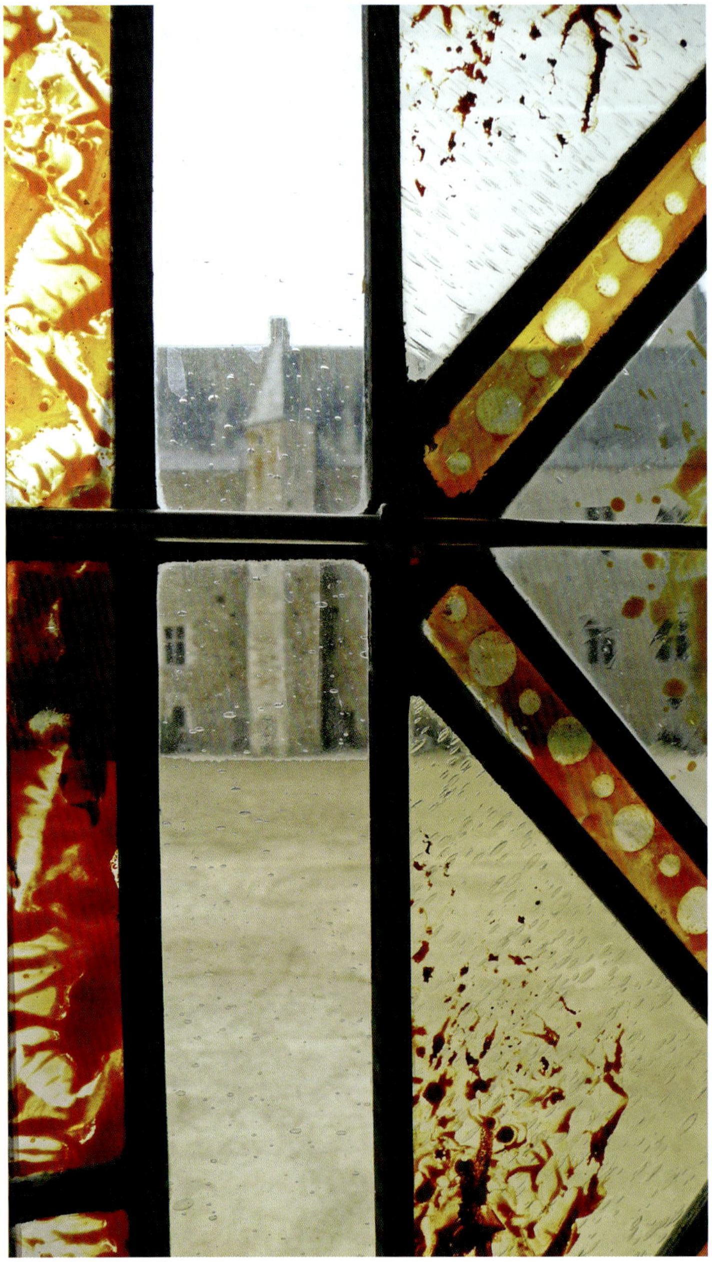

Sucinio Window 2007, Photograph, 8 x 10 inches

MAKING A POEM

Words heard before

Sounds spoken in another time

Nothing at all becomes something

Mystery upon magic

Someone is listening

2007

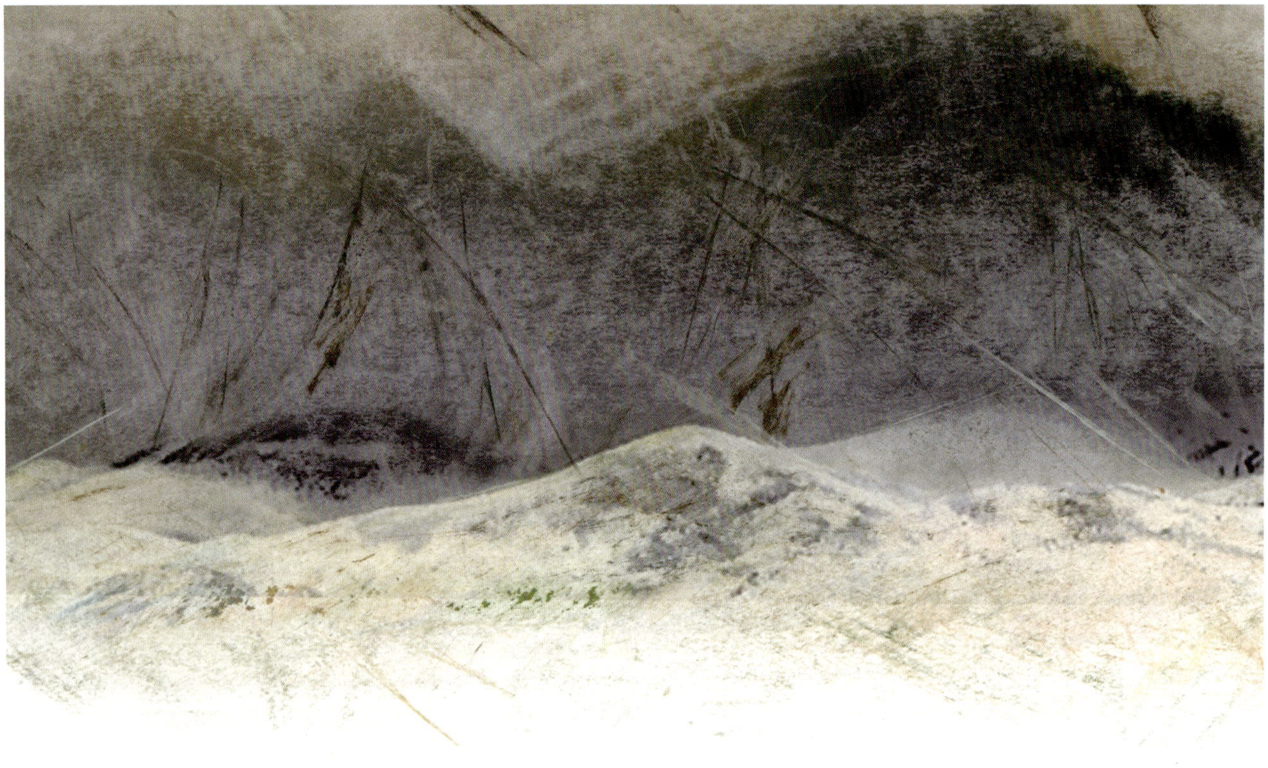

Storm in the Sangres 2006, Modified photograph, conte crayon, conte pencil, 10 x 6 inches

STORM AT DUSK

Clouds banked black against the less black mountains
Flying snow crossed by sun streaks
Afternoon light fractured
Into a winter rainbow

2006 Sangre de Cristo Mountains, Santa Fe

TEA

Soft golden green
Held by this shred of gentle burned earth,
Smelling of hillsides and the sunrise,
Giving up the bitter-clean taste of the morning –
The silky light rises to warm me.

Holding sunlight forever
In tiny black bits
Whispering in the darkness
Longing to set free the golden being
It has been from the beginning.

1984

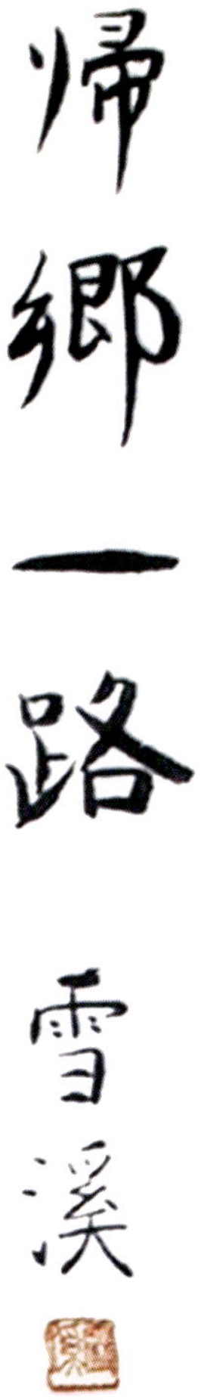

ONE PATH HOME

KIKYO ICHI RO

Alone the old crane stands
In the morning stillness
Long feathers rustling amidst brittle stems
Eyes sweeping the sky
Considering the path home

New Year's Day 2007

Recreated from the author's original Japanese

Calligraphy–Kikyo Ichi Ro Korean ink on paper, 1974, 3 x 12 inches

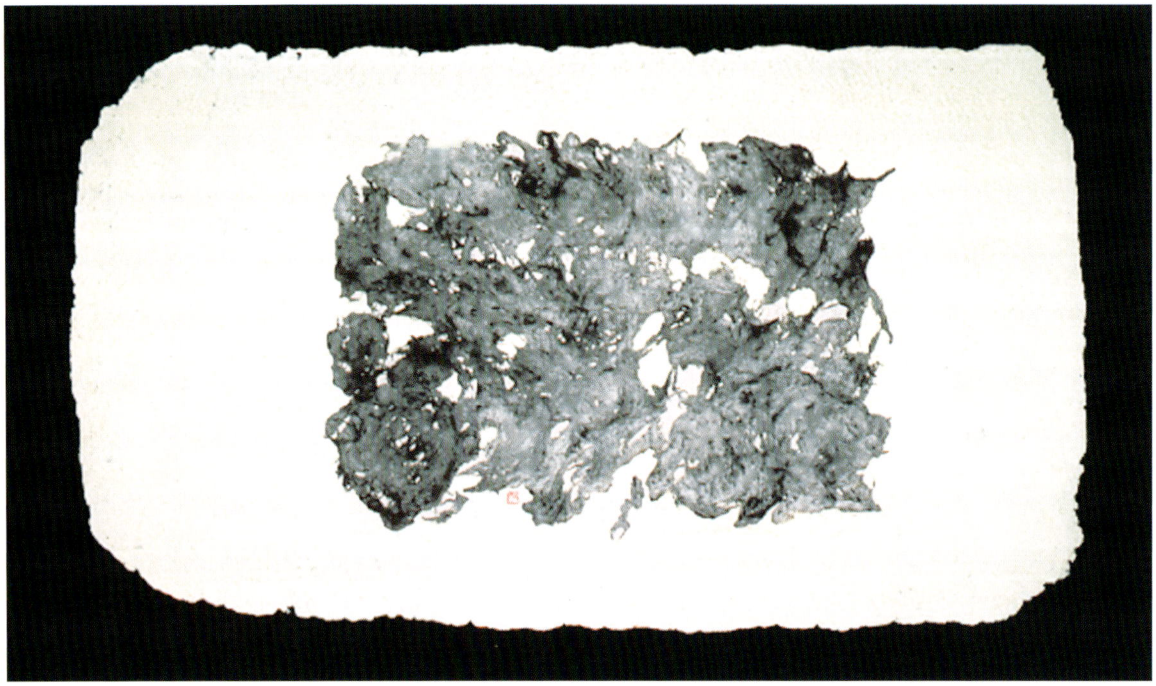

Time and Again 1987, Low relief sculpture. Linen fiber, mulberry paper, sumi ink, 35 x 20 x 1 inches

PAPER AND INK

Ink: blackest love

Paper: whitest host

Trees: living breathing green
            home for birds' songs
                        worms' love

Cut blasted burned charred

Ready to accept the embrace of our words.

Paper: whitest host

Ink: blackest love

WEST VIRGINIA GALAXIES

In West Virginia
The red stripes of the afternoon sky
Meet the evening over the village novas.

Each point starting to shine in the new dark is connected,
Sending strands of light to one another.

The last of the winter afternoon
Shines on the glittering remains of summer's fertility,
Igniting the overpowering geometry
Of frozen irrigation circles inside their square girdles.
The ponds here and there are still now,
Showing the last motion of fall.

Towns, hamlets, farms –
Some are filled with blue and green light
Gentle against the newly black sky
And the blacker night around them.
Some are vivid orange-yellow beacons
Brushing bold against the winter ground,
A few glow white with halogen
        Some sharp as pins
        Some a little blurred in the center.

Still there is a trace of red sky beyond the grounded world.

Some places have everything just right

2006

NEBRASKA SUNRISE

On the verge of a pond, grass glimmers with rime.
The thin ice cracks in tatters as the temperature rises a few degrees.
Early cold sunlight seeps across the eastern plain
And lends its energy to the half-frozen water.
New mists vaporize in a minute
Like crushed diamonds
Rising on the still silent air
Awakening the loons.

2006

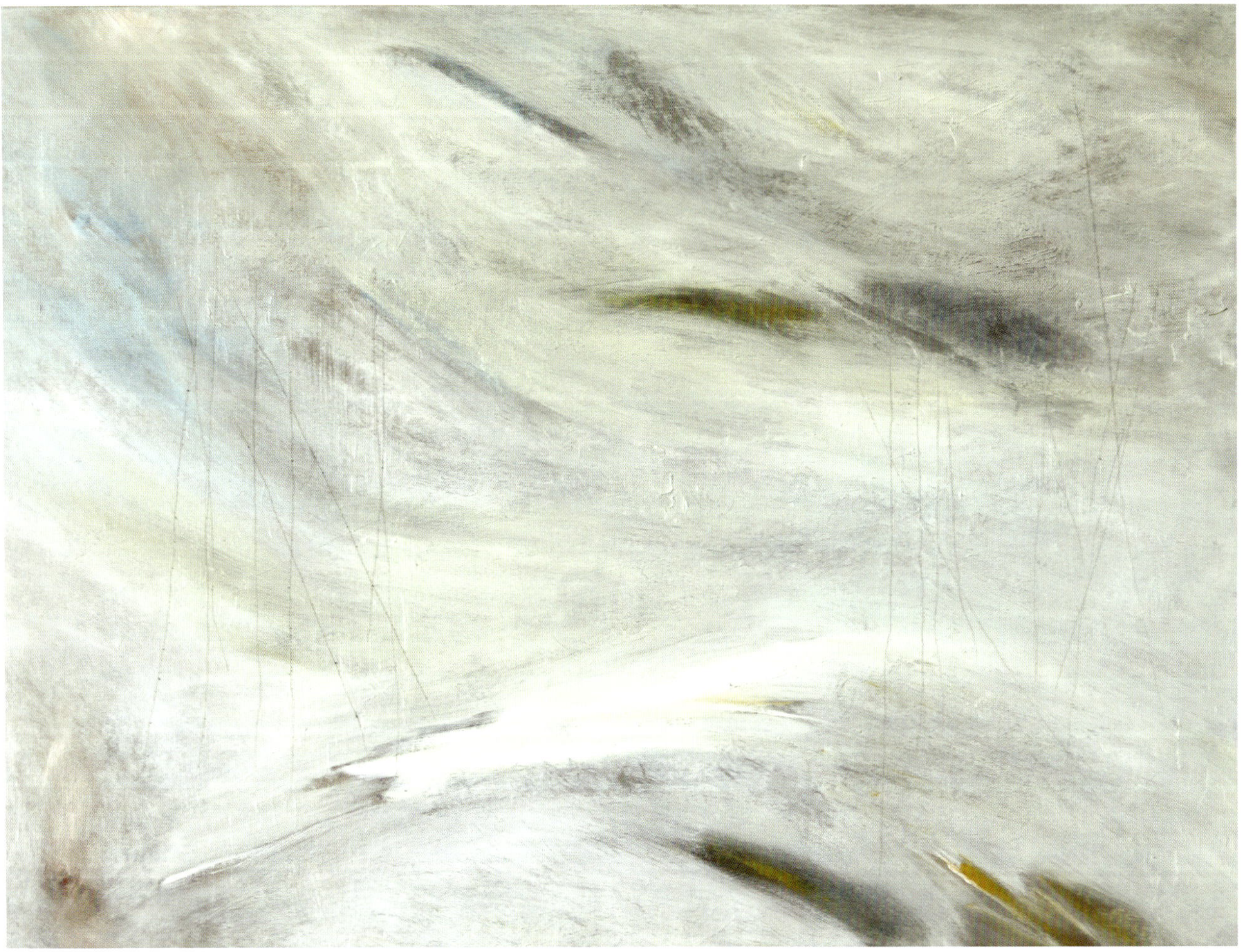

Brittany Morning 2007, Oil on canvas, 30 x 23 inches

IN TRANSIT

The night draws each body
Over the moonless horizon.
Jupiter rises
To dazzle the stars,
Orbiting toward dawn.

April 2007

THREE NOTE HELLO

Cole Porter told us to face the music and dance.

Moonlight and music and summer romance

Were absent

When you rang the doorbell.

You said,

Hello,

In three notes,

Your song rising, rolling a little lower,

Ending with a raised eyebrow.

You said hello in three notes

Looping down to announce

You were here

Rising to ask

Was I there?

Dancing came later.

2007

STONE MUSIC

In a pond summer rain is falling.
The black stones, worn smooth in the stream,
Click against each other
In our pockets

1975/2006 Recreated from the author's original Japanese

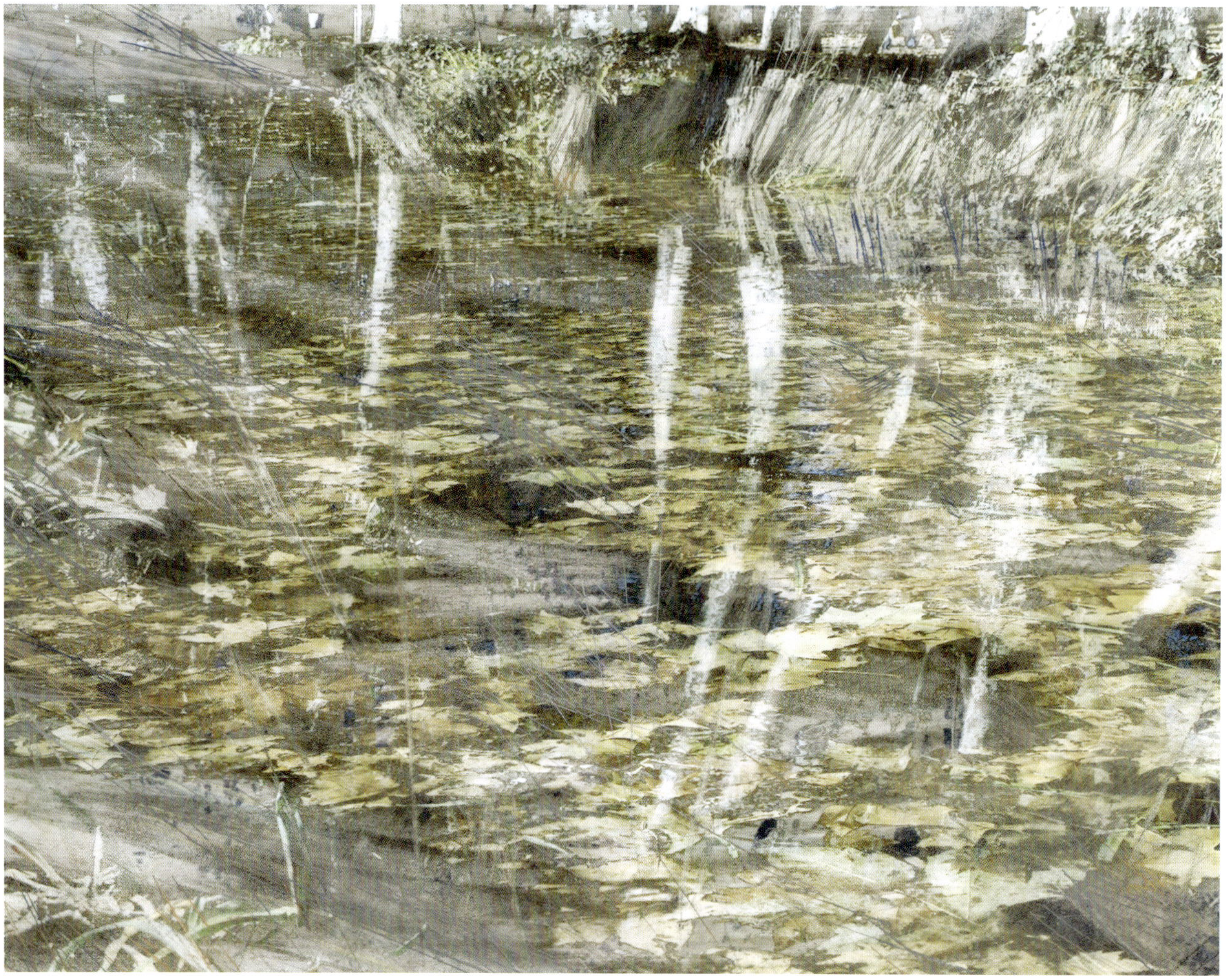

At the Embankment, Girona 2006, Modified photograph, mixed media, 8 x 10 inches

AT THE EMBANKMENT

A stone in the river
Washed smooth by twenty years' absence
Lies wet in the sunshine.

Heavy in my hand now
It lay gently in the muddy bed.
Its igneous body contains
The history of the world.

A wader in this stream
May step in the icy flow
And fall against its solid actuality.

1991

SUNDAY BREAKFAST

You woke this morning
Meaning to smile
Your eyes squinting in the glare of hoarse clouds.

You woke this morning
Meaning to sing
Wanting a great fall of trumpets and beautiful brassy noise.

But your heart had laryngitis
And whispered a softer song instead.

So squinting and humming a little sharp
You made coffee
And toast with cheese and honey.

1985

POSTAL SERVICE

Your unwritten letter

Unstamped

Unsealed

Unfolded in my heart

Says nothing at all.

1987

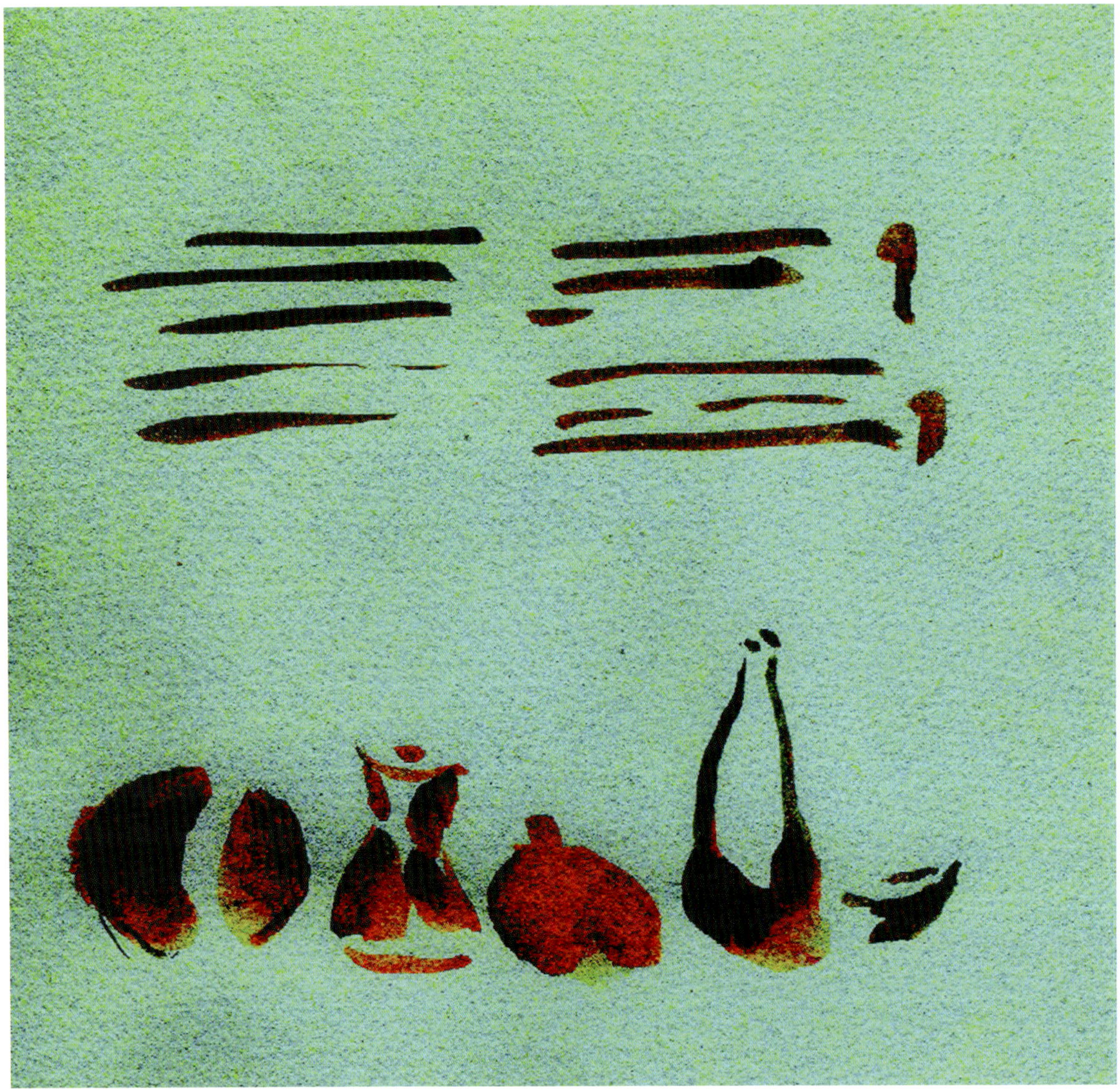

Lumiere: Contrevent avec Fruit 2003, Sumie painting, digitally modified, 8 x 8 inches

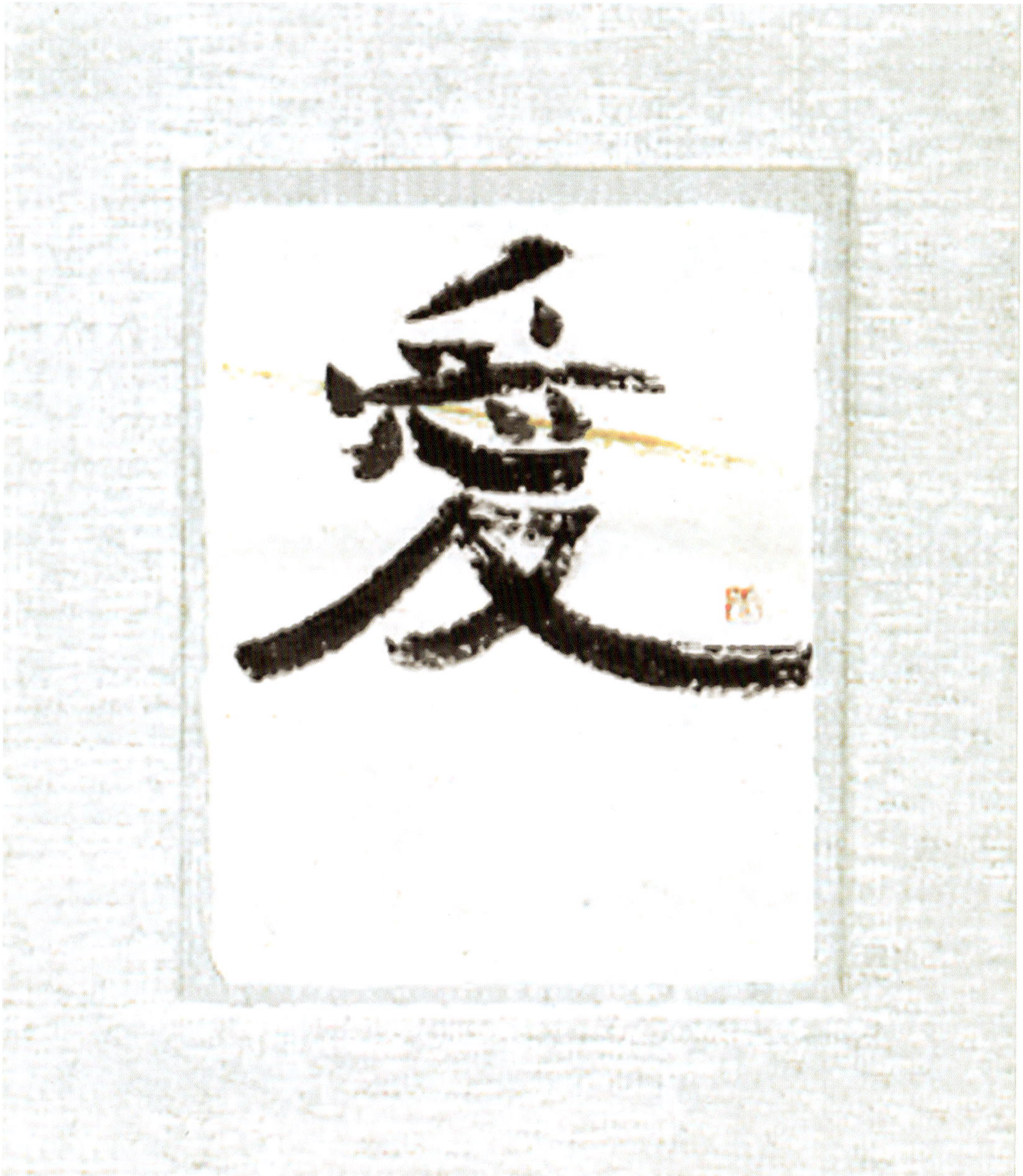

Calligraphy–Love 1985, Sumi ink and Chinese yellow on paper made by the artist, 14.5 x 12.5 inches

MIDNIGHT BLUES

The heat has reawakened
An army of flies.
Unwillingly I stay awake

And see the moon set.

2004

CHANGE OF SEASON

Waterfall

Falling

Water

Running down the cheeks of the hills.

Coldspring

Spring

Rain

Has fallen into the cleft of the rock.

Airspray

Air

Sprays of icy fragrance

Tears blown over the sky.

1998

SHAKUHACHI

The sound of the bamboo falls over the valley

Snowflakes of sound on the sierra

Riding the wind

Embracing the air

Leaving crystals of silence

2006 Recreated from the author's original Spanish

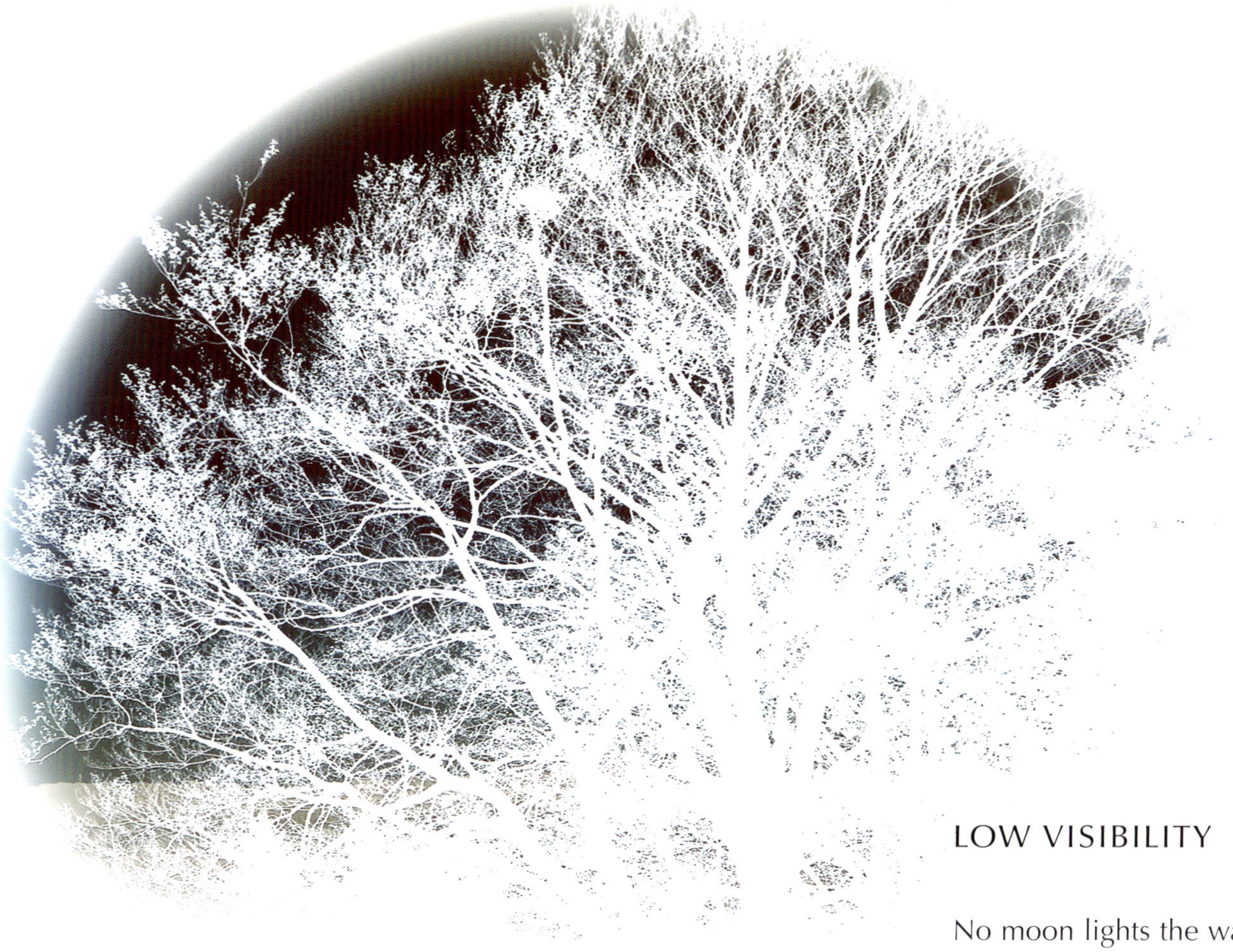

LOW VISIBILITY

No moon lights the way
Breath in the cold air
is just visible –
        Clouds rising to the clouds –
We guess where the road goes

Low Visibility 2007, Modified photograph with text, 8 x 10 inches

WHERE THE FLOWERS HAVE GONE

Armistice Day 11 November 2004

Wreaths of roses blood red

Garlands of chrysanthemums

More yellow than the sun.

    Talk of honor

    Talk of sacrifice

    Talk of harm's way

Then shoot.

2004

FEVER

Hot faces

Hot words

A fever of hate

A fire in the blood

Shoot hack rip rape

Slash burn bomb

What else can you do?

What else can we do?

2007

UNSETTLED CONDITIONS

Sun tomorrow
Followed by cloudy days
Then rain
Breezy conditions
Small craft warnings
Large lakes advisory

Turbulence in the upper atmosphere

Any time is the time
To go to war.

2007

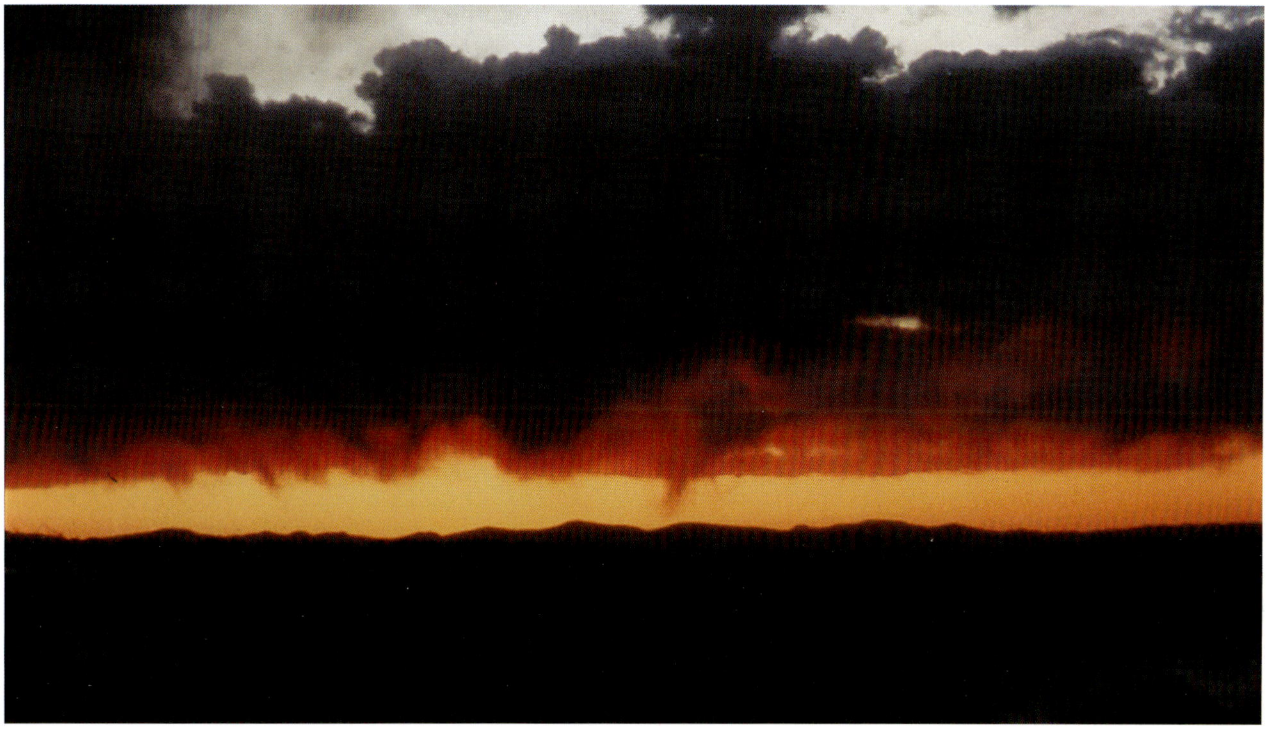

Cerro Grande Fire 2003, Photograph, 8 x 10 inches

SNOWSTORM

Cold wind
Scraps of sky
Cracked out of the clouds
Cold ground
Dull with brown rigidity

Coming soon
The snow we've longed for

2006

MAPLE LEAF

A maple leaf blazes through the day

Then falls to rest

On a stone in the stream

1987

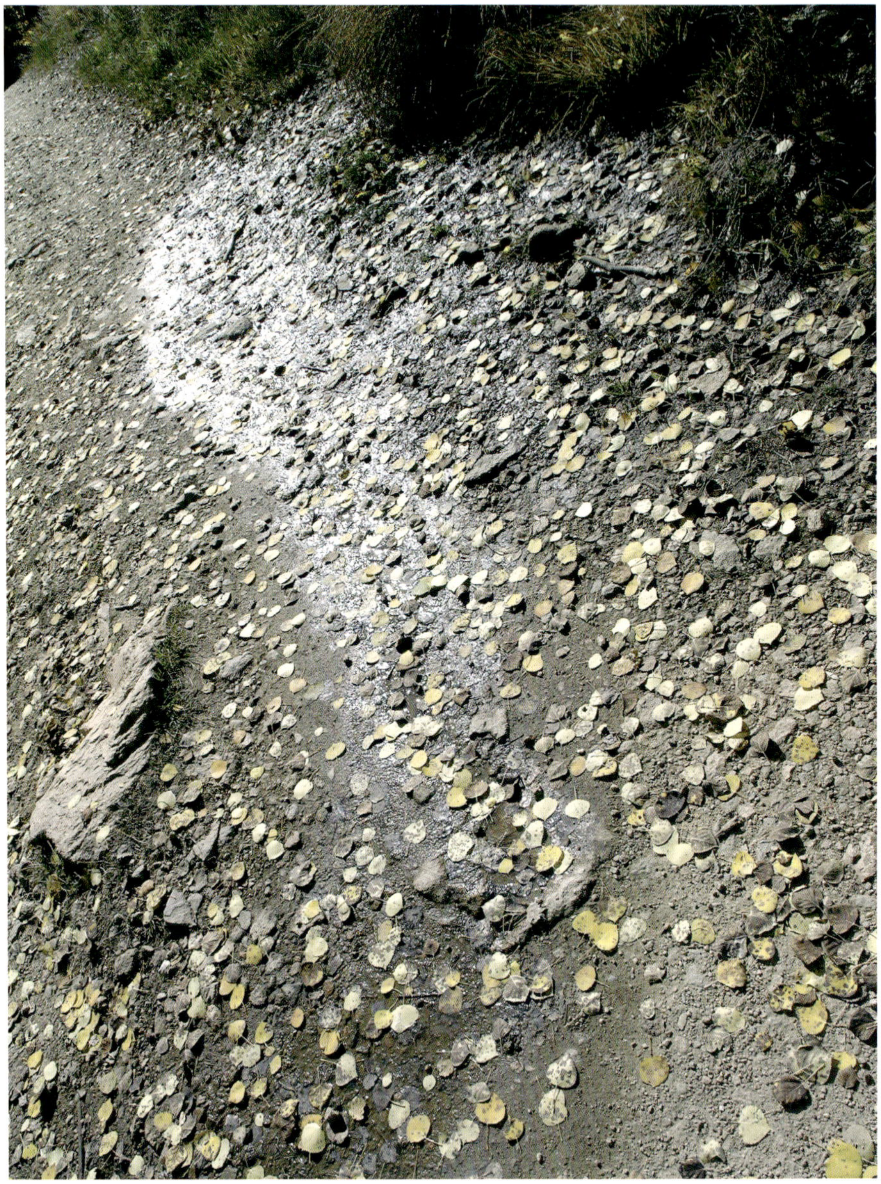

Fallen Leaves, Aspen Vista 2006, Photograph, 8 x 10 inches

MUFFLED CLAPPERS

Each leaf sounds one time

Over and over

Until finally we hear them clearly.

2006

SCHOOL DAYS

First of September

Girls' hair blowing across their eyes

Boys proudly wearing T-shirts a little too small

Men with glasses and important briefcases

Women with babies and books and seriousness on their laps

Promising lawyers, cool enterprisers –

Passionate zoologists, precise French speakers –

All dreaming

Couples and trios and quartets sit on the grass

Leaning toward and then away from each other

In a friendship-making dance

They talk about death and art and freedom and sex

And what kind of pizza to get

1987

AUGUST

The meadow is alight

Cicadas brush their wings in desperate lust

A dark-haired girl stops for a moment

Listening to the shadows

2006

56

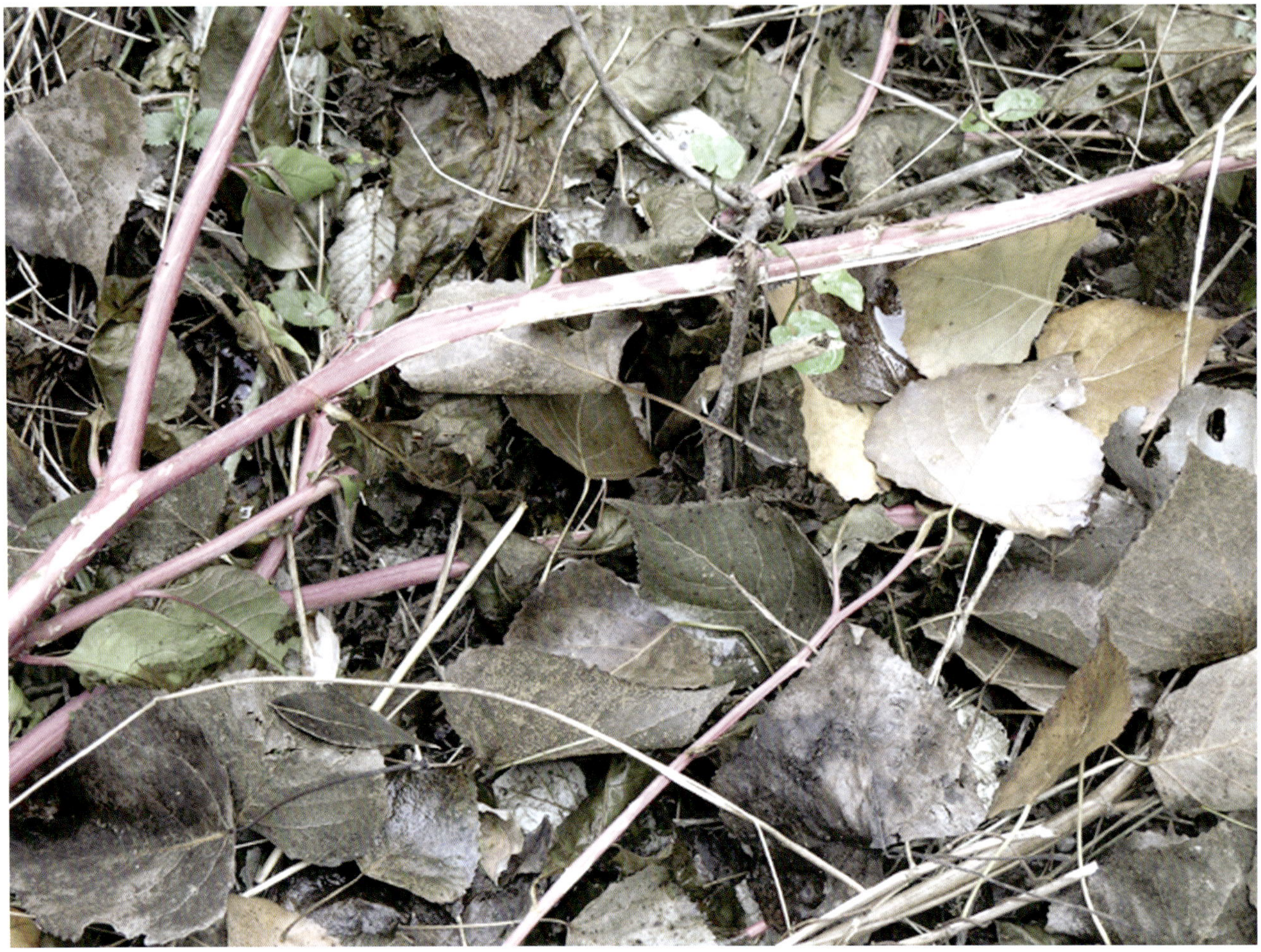

Red Twig 2004–5, Photograph, 8 x 10 inches

RED TWIG

Morning fog lifted its wet weight
And left the red twig
Shining in remembrance.

The clouds, in a prism of urgency,
Oblivious
Rush to the sea.

An insect passes almost silently
Lost in the litter of last summer.

2004

BRITTANY SPRING

Up past the atmosphere
Steaming breath and steaming coast
Meet the streaming foggy sky.

Rough edged clouds
Remember the cold sea
Where they were born.

The sky is suddenly blue
Above the pitching, stretching ocean of cloud,
Glowing clean in the high afternoon light,

So brilliant
That you have to squint
Or turn away for just a moment.

Ahead, banks, piles, mountains of air
Holding all the ocean's blue
And the tangerine-gold edges of evening.

Maybe it will rain again tomorrow.

2007

TRAVELING

You are so far away

Finding yourself in front of snowy smoking mountains

Brushing out of your hair the dust of miracles

Closing your eyes in the face of the six-o'clock sun.

1985

Yellow Tree in Fog, Montserrat
2004–5, Photograph
8 x 10 inches

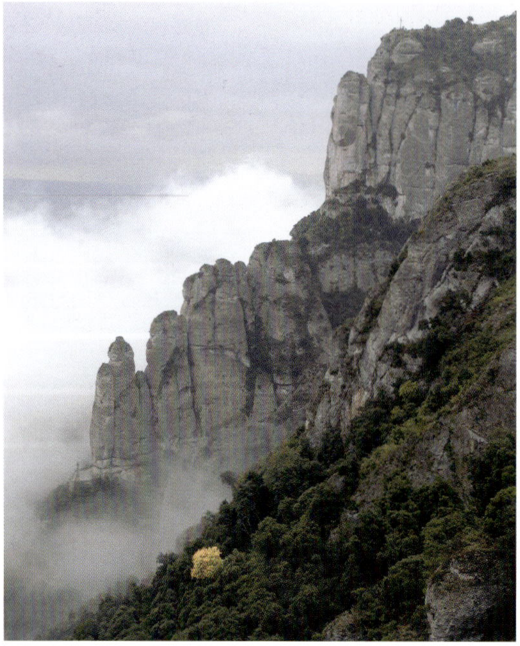

MONTSERRAT

Red walls, shining wood floor, bright lights–
A room full of things.

two long white glowing wedding dresses
sequins, embroidery, gathered stitching
covering silk petticoats and sheer linings.

sleeves touching the white silk
a very short suit of black wool–
a young brother to accompany the bride?
a stranger?

Brass hooks hold
small shoes

plastic flowers

an infant's yellow bib

a summery straw hat with silk flowers around the crown

a tiny girl's starched pink dress

white rickrack pristine

no dribbles from a meal of applesauce.

Past the corner more hooks.

And a shelf with

baskets

a brass box with a dark red velvet lining

a music box

Round the corner again

more plastic flowers

toys

photographs

crutches

sorrows

gratitude

and a sign

that says

that everything—all the objects—

are left behind

and may yet be reclaimed.

Outside people are passing by

RAIN RAIN

All this fine rainy day
Clouds have scudded in the wind
Chasing isobars of cold air
Across the spring jet stream.

1998

GHOST HOUSE AT THE BRIDGE

Dharma drama derrama

Words falling in the cascade of air

Lines found in any order

Reordered

Folded away

Found again

Foundering in the torrent

Found shelter

Sheltered the solitary reader in the rain.

2006

dharma: law or precepts ordering the universe (Buddhist)
drama: prose or verse telling a serious story (English)
derrama: spill, overflow, pour out (Spanish)

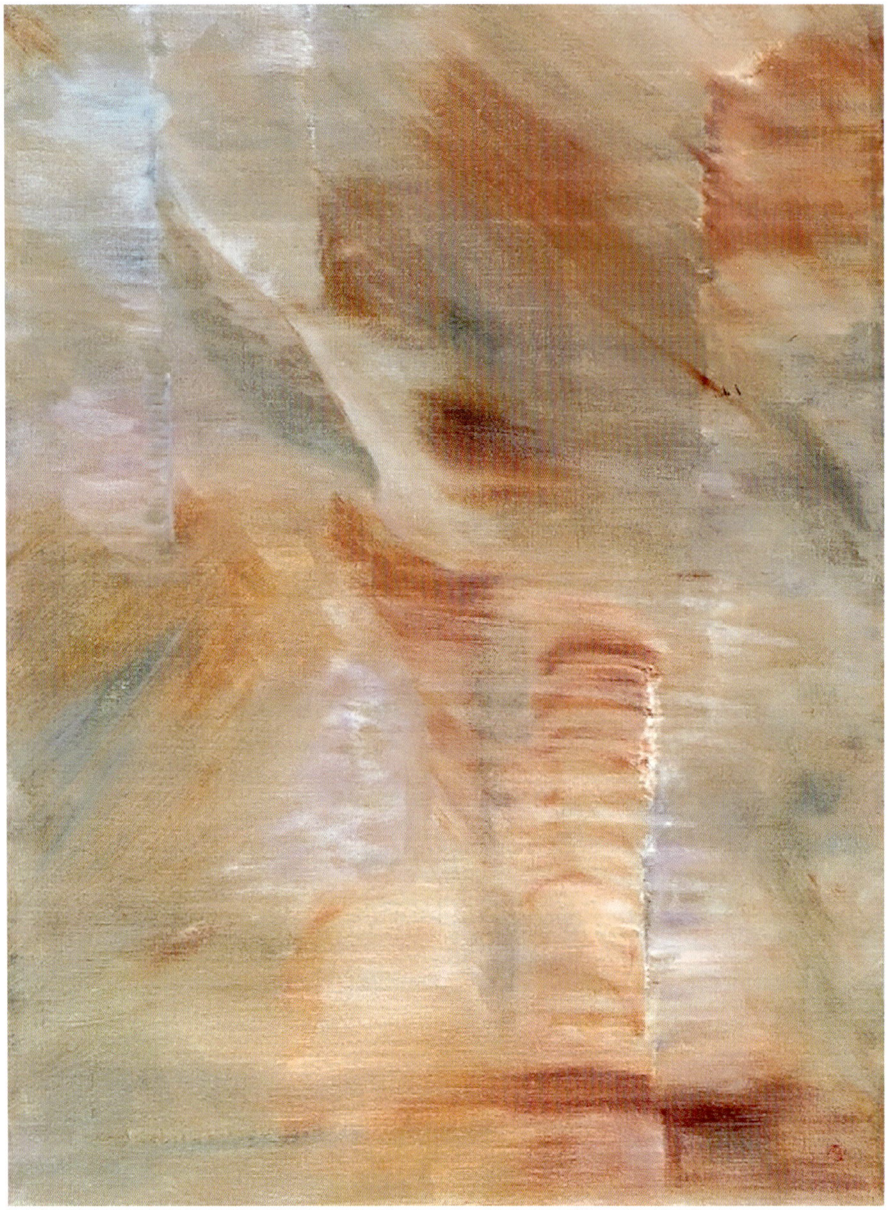

Arches 1997, Oil on linen, 29 x 21.5 inches

Maple Leaves, Ashfield Cemetery 2005, Photograph, 6 x 10 inches (right)

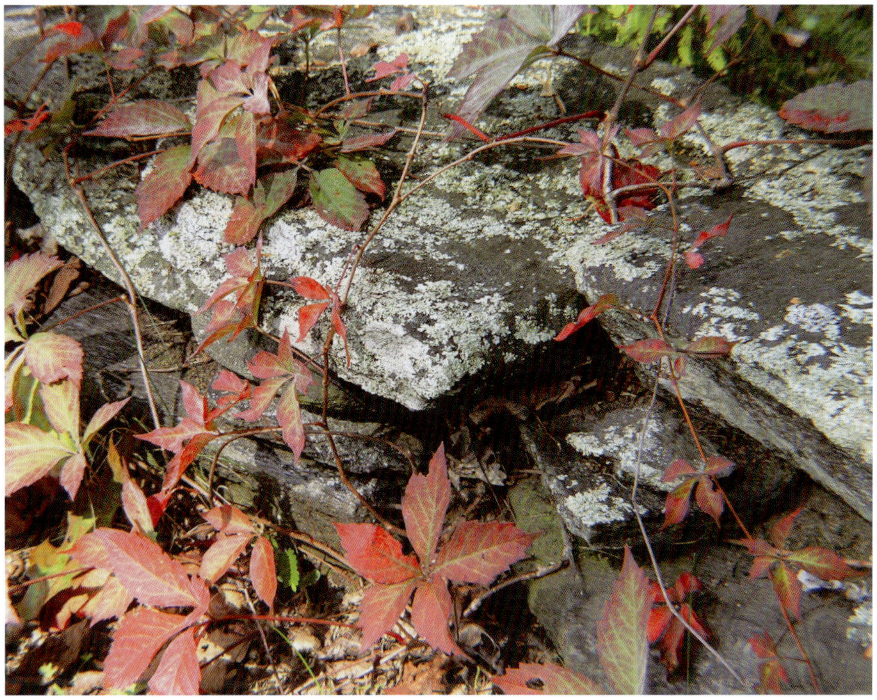

FOR LOVE OF RED

Red silk wet on the pine needles.

Maple and sumac glimmer red and dark along the road

But neither is as red

As the red wool blanket

In my blue room.

2000/2006

THAT DAY

If you knock your elbow against the edge of the door
The funny bone will send a thrill of shock
Right to your brain.

On that hot morning
Our eyes knocked.
In that instant
    every bone was funny
    every muscle laughing
    every hair breathless.

In the aftershock I kept touching
That electric pain
Leaning against the doorframe
Until my heart could move again.

1984

RICOCHET

At six o'clock the songs of swallows
Spill themselves through the air
Pushing themselves off imperturbable yellow stone walls.

Boulders, stuck fast forever,
Are disturbed in the echo.

1985/2004

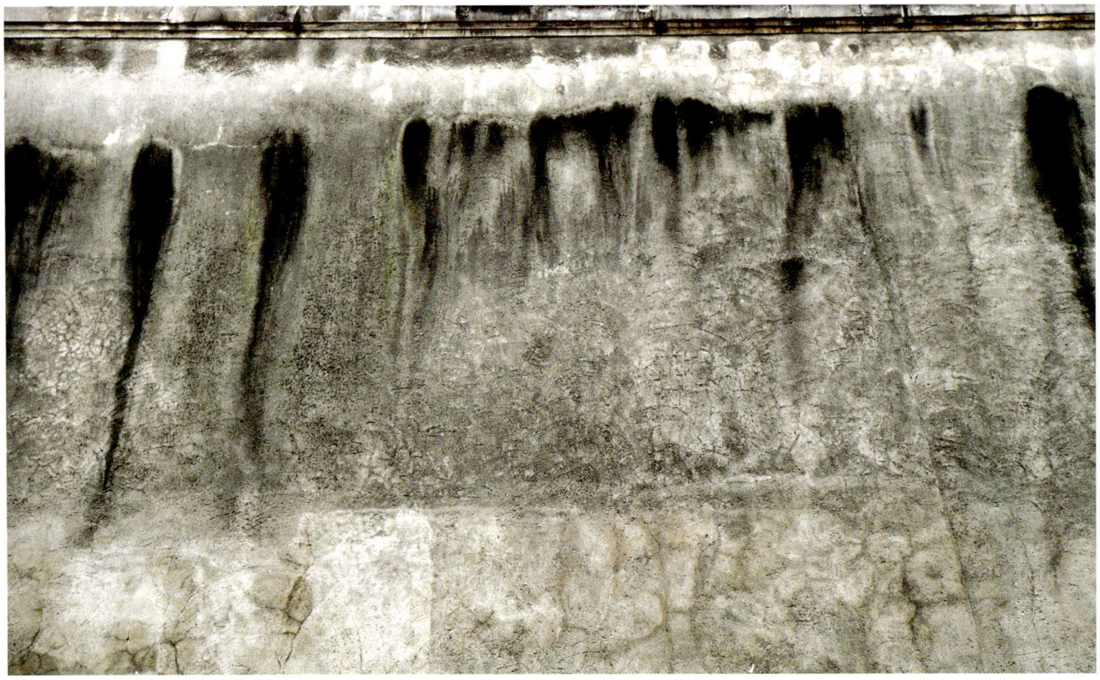

For ASKing

With no other proof but memory

Exists that moon blue eye,

A black curl creeping over the edge of an ear,

A smile committed to nothing more–or less–than that moment

Trusting an untrustworthy future.

1991

Falling Black, Le Marais 2007, Digitally modified print, 8 x 10 inches

SUMMER IDYLL

One note from a child's flute

Resting on the air

Like a swallow on the porch rail

1989

BRETON DAY

Pouring drizzle
Sheets of soft rain
Descending over the garden
Watery sunshine inundated again
By the cloudy rain rolling low on the landscape.

Stinging tiny droplets
Pass in windy torrents
Then lift again
Making room for the mists of morning.
All day every molecule drinks its fill.

At ten o'clock the daylight fades
And clouds wreathe the moon.
We'll see them again tomorrow.

2007

CLOUDS

Clouds blow high, born of our dust
Returning to caress us
In a silver fog.

2006

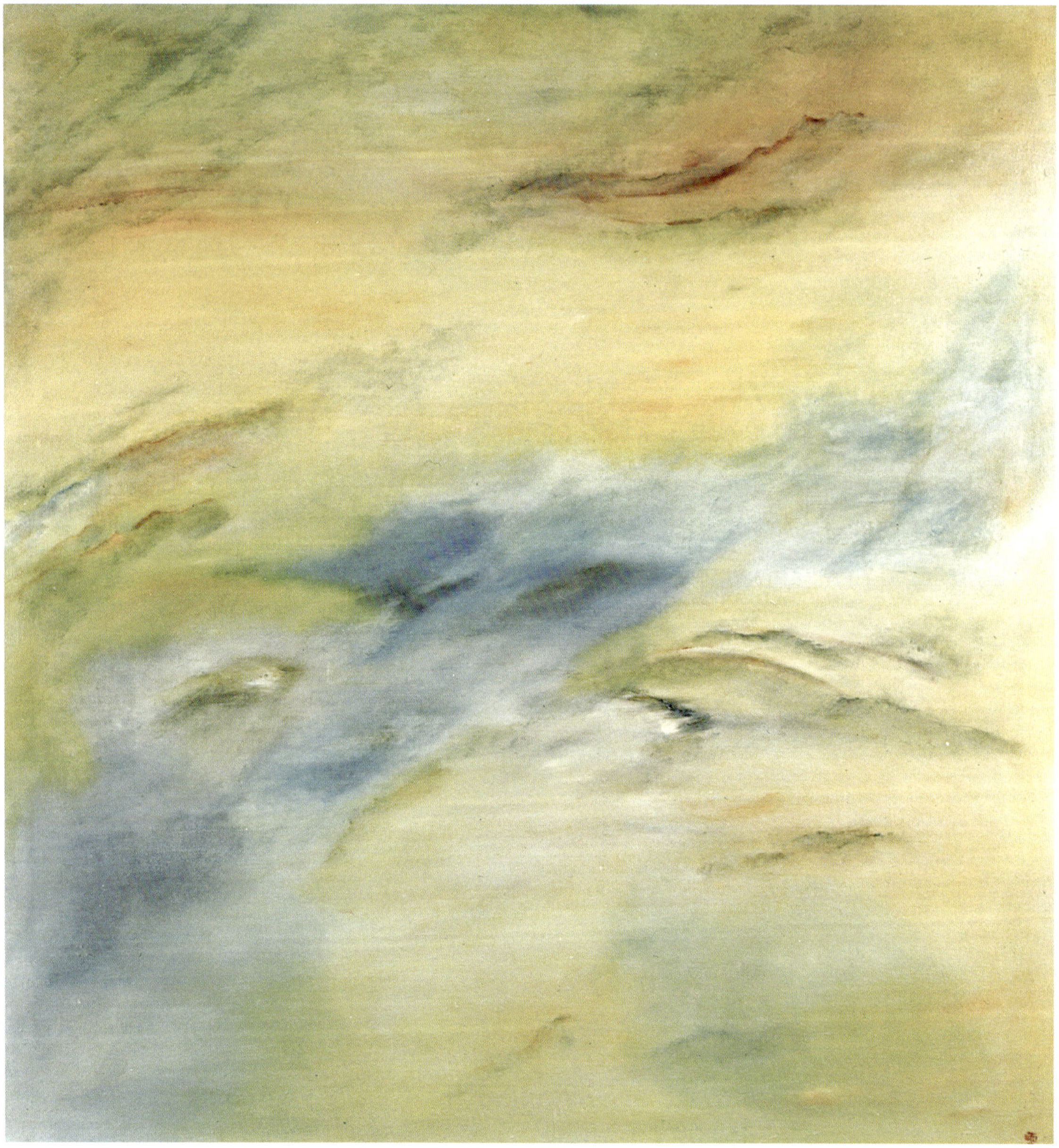

Composition in Yellow and Blue (Married Life) 1998, Oil on linen, 47 x 52 inches

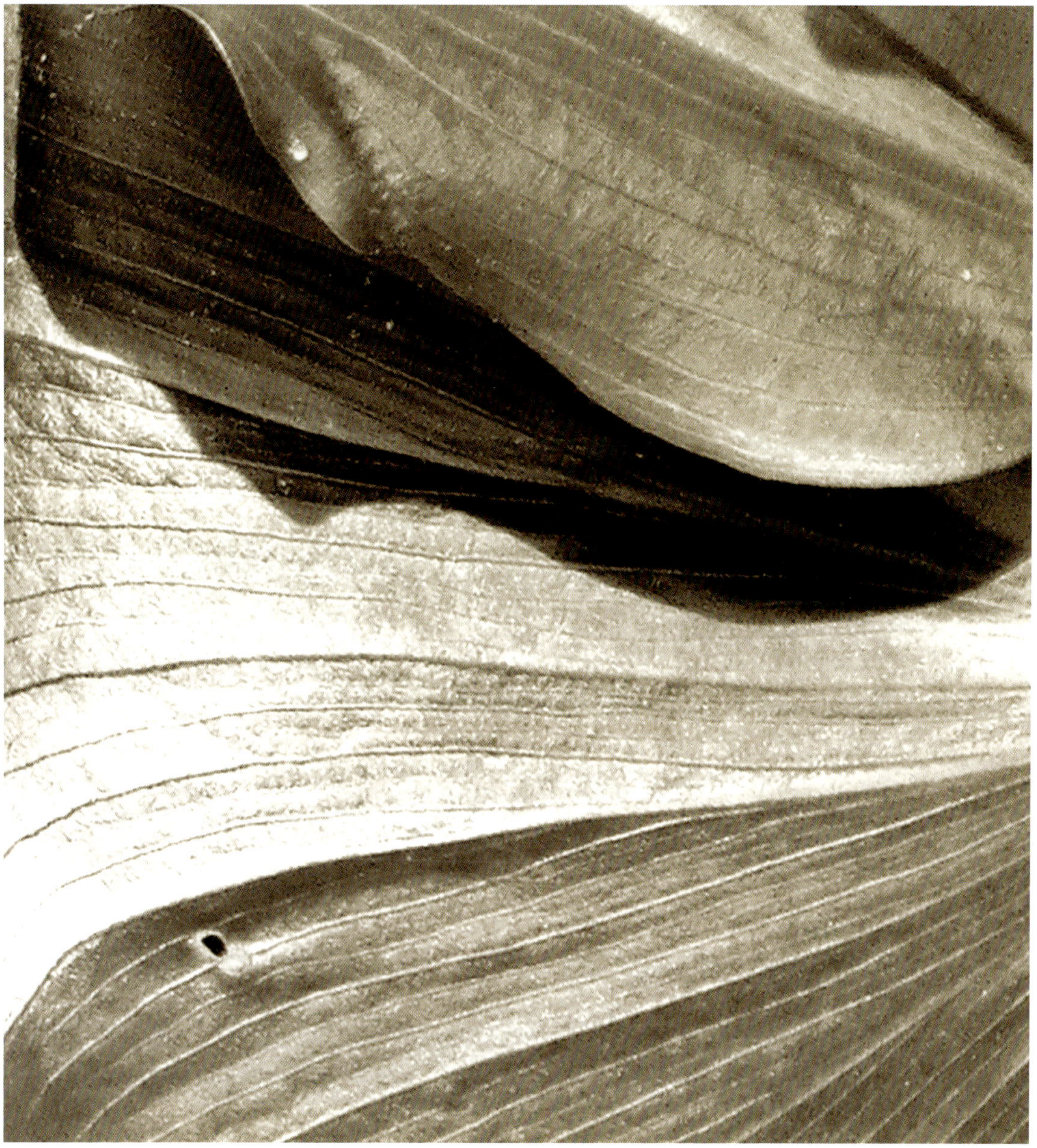

Rochefort Composition II 2007, Photograph, 7 x 7 inches

AT SANTA MARIA DEL MAR, BARCELONA

Body of light

Bending on the shallow steps

Lying prone on the cold beautiful stone

Curling up the wall

Climbing toward the arch of heaven

HUMID NIGHT AIR

At this hour, before sunrise,
Empty and without colors,
The invisible grass is touched
Only by dew.

2007

76

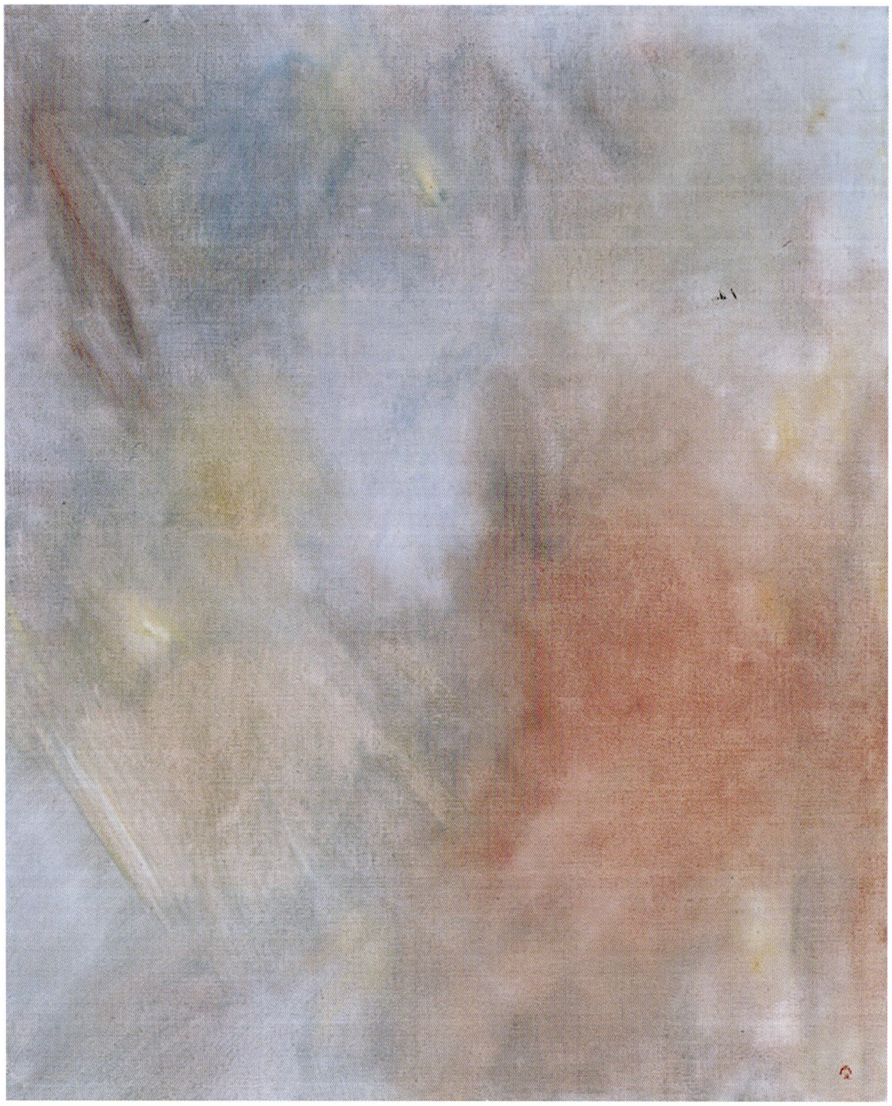

Blue in Red 1997, Oil on linen, 40 x 32 inches; the first oil painting

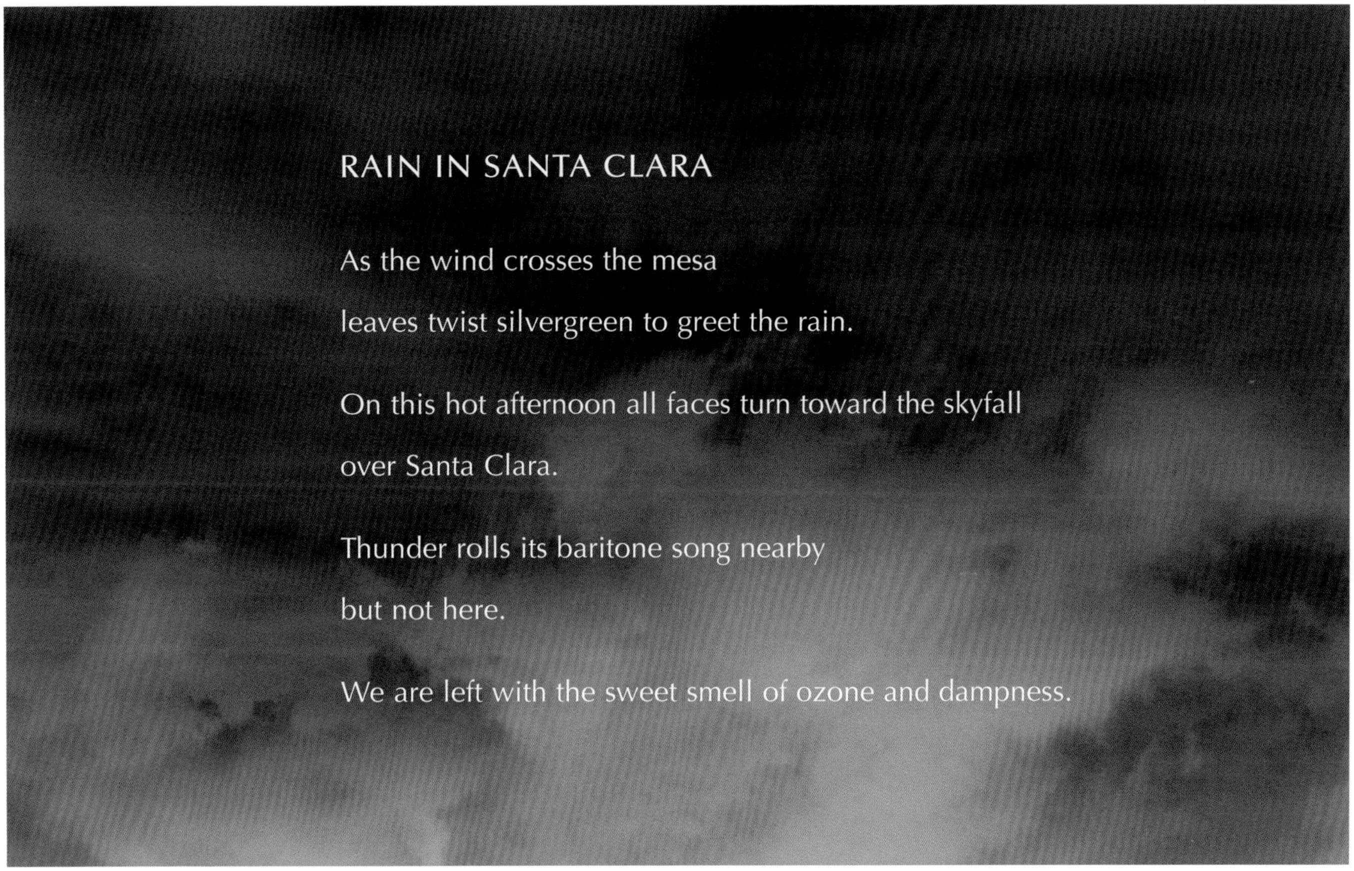

Rain in Santa Clara 2007, Modified photograph with text, 8 x 8 inches

QUIET FOG

Quiet fog, sliding over the roof,
Shapeless,
Colors hidden,
Almost silent.

In the deepening dusk
Rain falls through the fog,
Across the stones.

In the silence
Water drips on the forest mouse.
Do you hear the splash?

Somewhere near
A song is heard.

1998

FULL MOON

Last night

A bird crossed in the path of moonlight.

The shadow ran over the white wall

And was lost in the window.

2004

NIGHT TABLE

Dusk eases its way
Past the meridian.
The sky is dark.

Beside the bed
    essentials crowd the night table
        clock
        lamp
        radio
        novel
        eyeglasses

    a small pitcher with a sprig of lilac
        a breath of the spring garden
        panicles already drooping
        like tired eyelids

    tea in a china cup without a saucer
        smelling of faraway hills
        spices
        journeys and dreams

    a pencil next to the leather notebook
        the scent of trees
        a whiff of the life they once had
        waiting for a new life of words

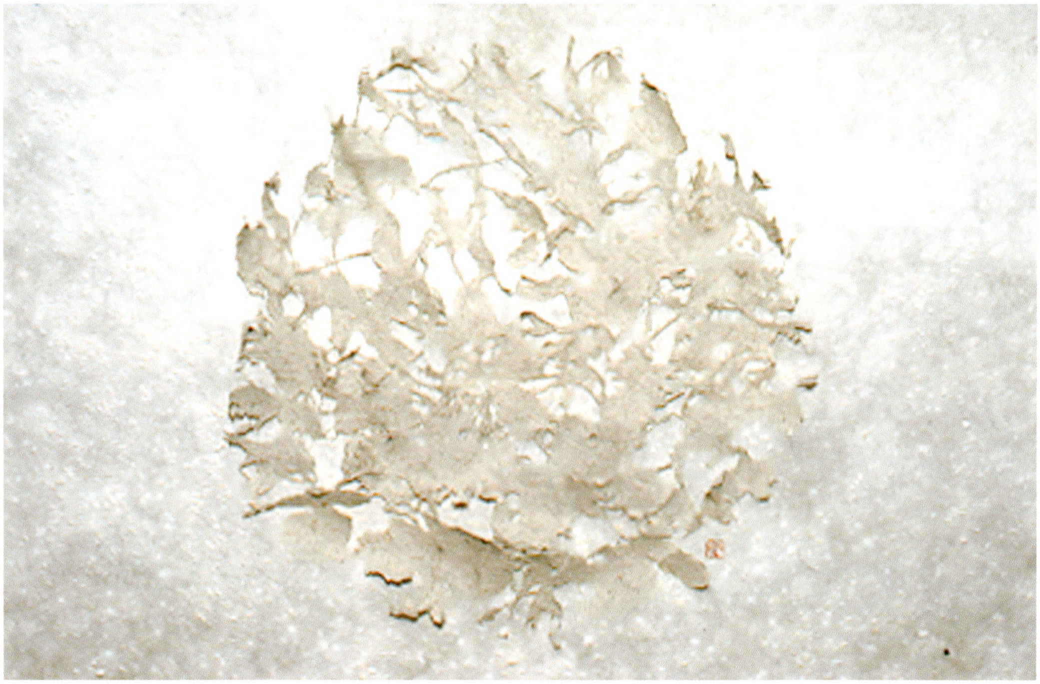

a photograph

remembrance of a sweet day

the aspens glowing

your smile alight

Sleeping is a temporary death

So few things

Awaken us to this life

2007

Lo que dibuja la noche 1987, Low relief sculpture, 48 x 36 x 1.25 inches
Linen and mulberry papers made by the artist

CALLING

In the freezing sunshine
Each heavy green leaf of the magnolia tree
Turns a bit toward the trunk.

The sap is still this brilliant day.
The sun shines hard on the morning ice.

Don't you hear the cold wind call?

2007

ACROBATICS

A single drop in the deluge
Twisting in the cascade of air
          Falling
                    Turning
                              Returning

By chance somersaults into the sea.

1984/2006 recreated from the author's original Spanish

REMEMBERING AN APRIL DAY

at a cemetery

In a quiet room
On a dark table with fat legs
There is a box–
          big enough to hold picnic for a family,

Outside in the sunshine, standing in the grass
My heart is screaming
                              speechless

Ah, my beloved, we are silent.

2004

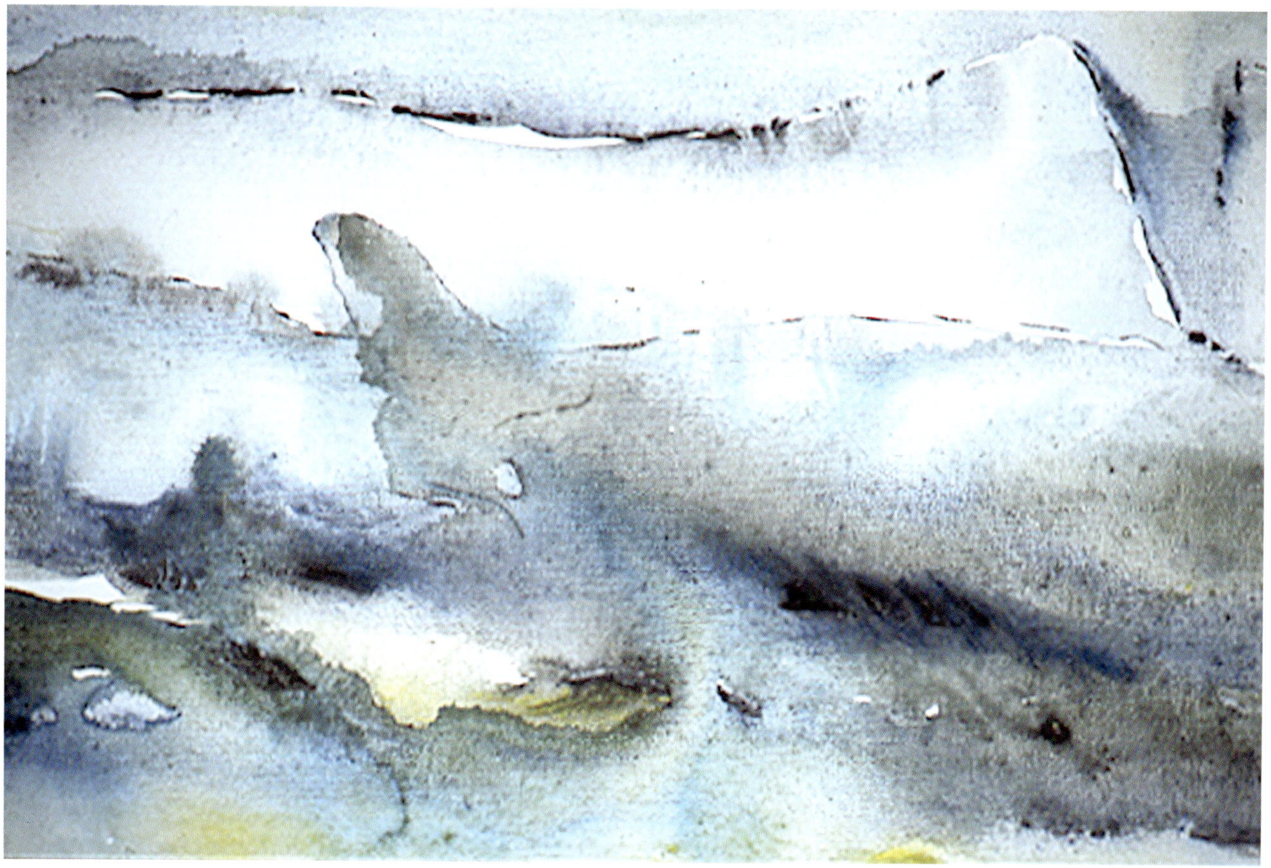

Montañas sin nombre 1987, Watercolor and inks on canvas, 33 x 27 inches

BEDTIME STORY

I was dreaming of aspens
        Of making a bed.
        He said it will look pretty
But it will never hold up like that.

I made a picture of a bed, he made a picture of a bed.
        Four almost straight posts at the corners
        Three long trees on the sides.
Head to rest heads against, foot to hold it together.

Tree trunks sanded, polished, waxed
        Knots smoothed away
        Until they were just shadows
Memories of the branches

The aspen sawdust smelled
        Of forest and sap
        And sprayed out from the saw
Catching in our hair and eyelashes and sweaty skin.

Some assembly required.
        The pieces are fitted together
        Not quite perfectly
The long rails turn of their own accord sometimes

The first night the frame of head and foot and rails
    Sat on the floor around the mattress
    A crib for a new marriage
Next day the platform raised the quilted box

And dropped it again

More support was drawn up,
    Modified, built.
    We asked ourselves,
"Would the center hold?"

Now this old bed glows with so many polishings of wax
    Scratches gouged here and there
    Wood still soft,
As if it has just been interrupted as it grew.

Glowing in the morning
    As early sun sends a knife of light into the room
Glowing at midnight
    As the moon changes from evening gold to night white

Still holding together for now.

2007

GREEN BAMBOO

Imperceptible wind

Moves long green bamboo leaves

Across old black bark–

An inky brush in the Spanish air.

This almost tropical grass

Bending to the ground

Is cousin to upright bright Korean stalks,

Now in October

    Ready to give up their green life

    For the leafless windy winter.

2004

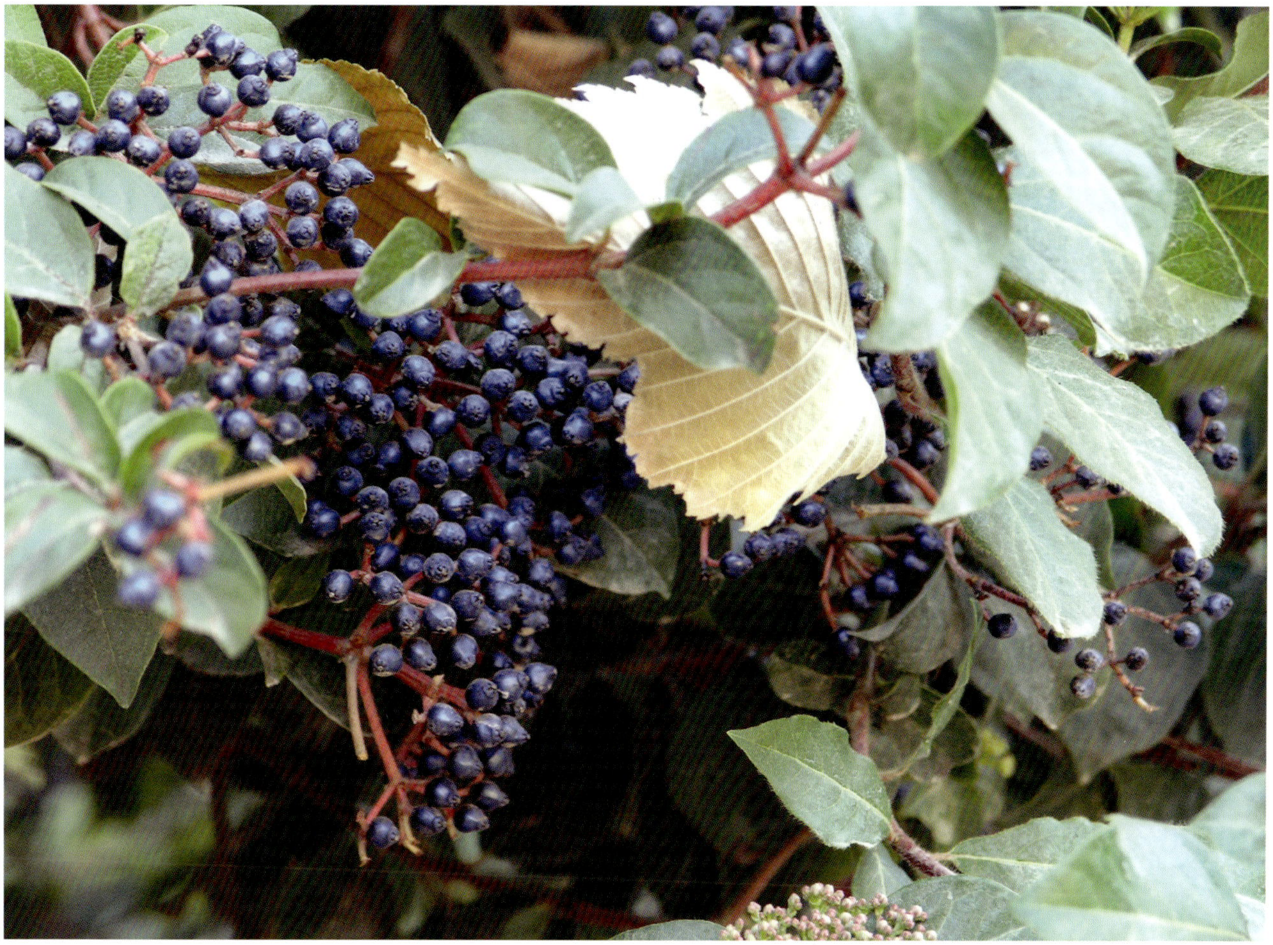

Grapes, El Partal, La Alhambra, Granada 2004, Photograph, 8 x 10 inches

JUNE GARDEN

Hardy perennial lilies
Do not need lifting.
Tall and graceful,
They like the sun.
They are dependable year after year.

Peonies are slow to take hold
But once established
Live in their beds
For centuries.

Iris quite quickly
Have great masses of beauty
But must be uprooted from time to time
Or die of exuberance.

1998

COLOR OF RED WINE

He said,

You get what you deserve
And you don't get what you don't deserve

Owing gratitude to no one
Except yourself, of course.

I am grateful to him for saying so
Reminding me
What didn't happen

2004

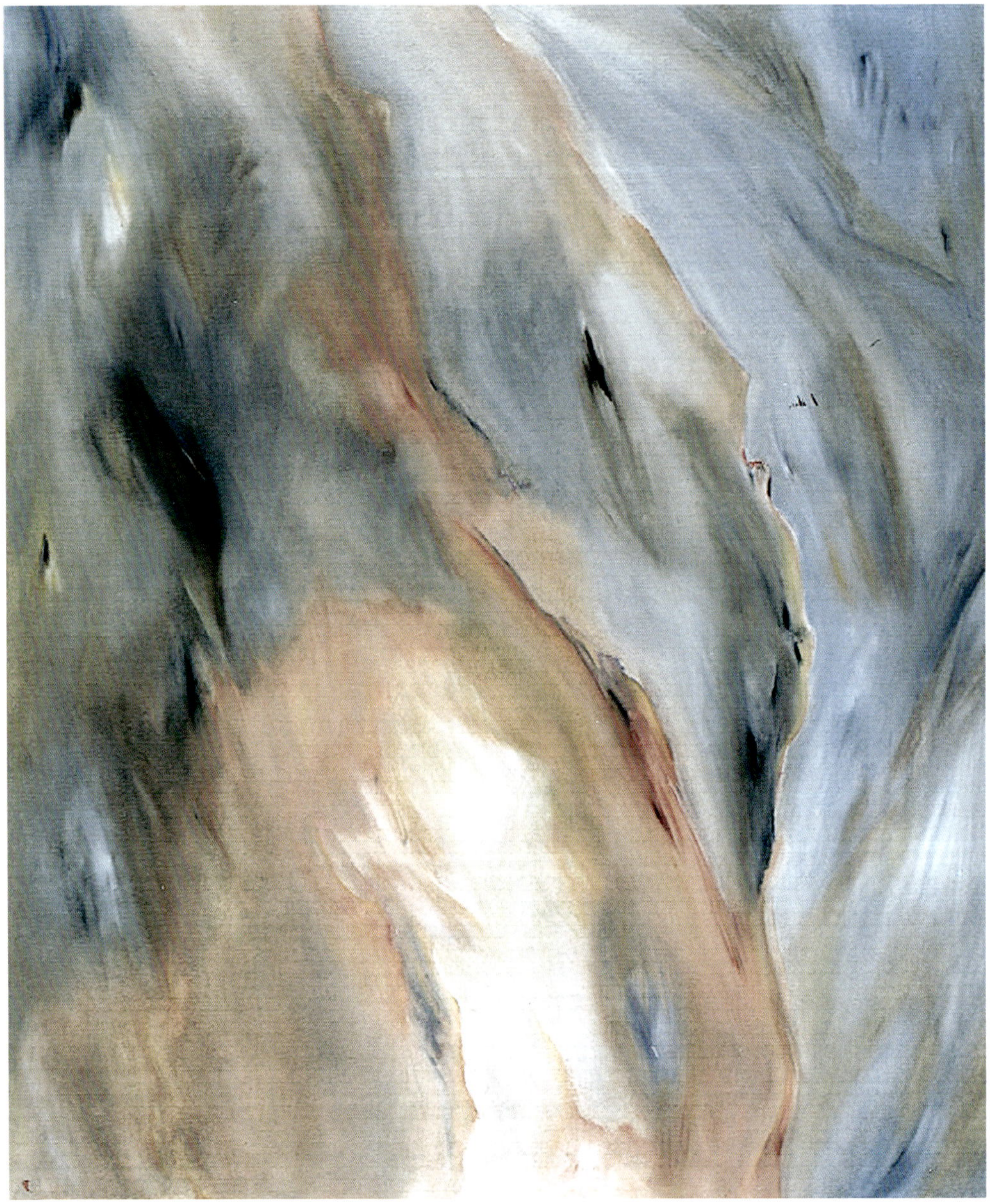

Anticipation 1998, Oil on linen, 52 x 43 inches

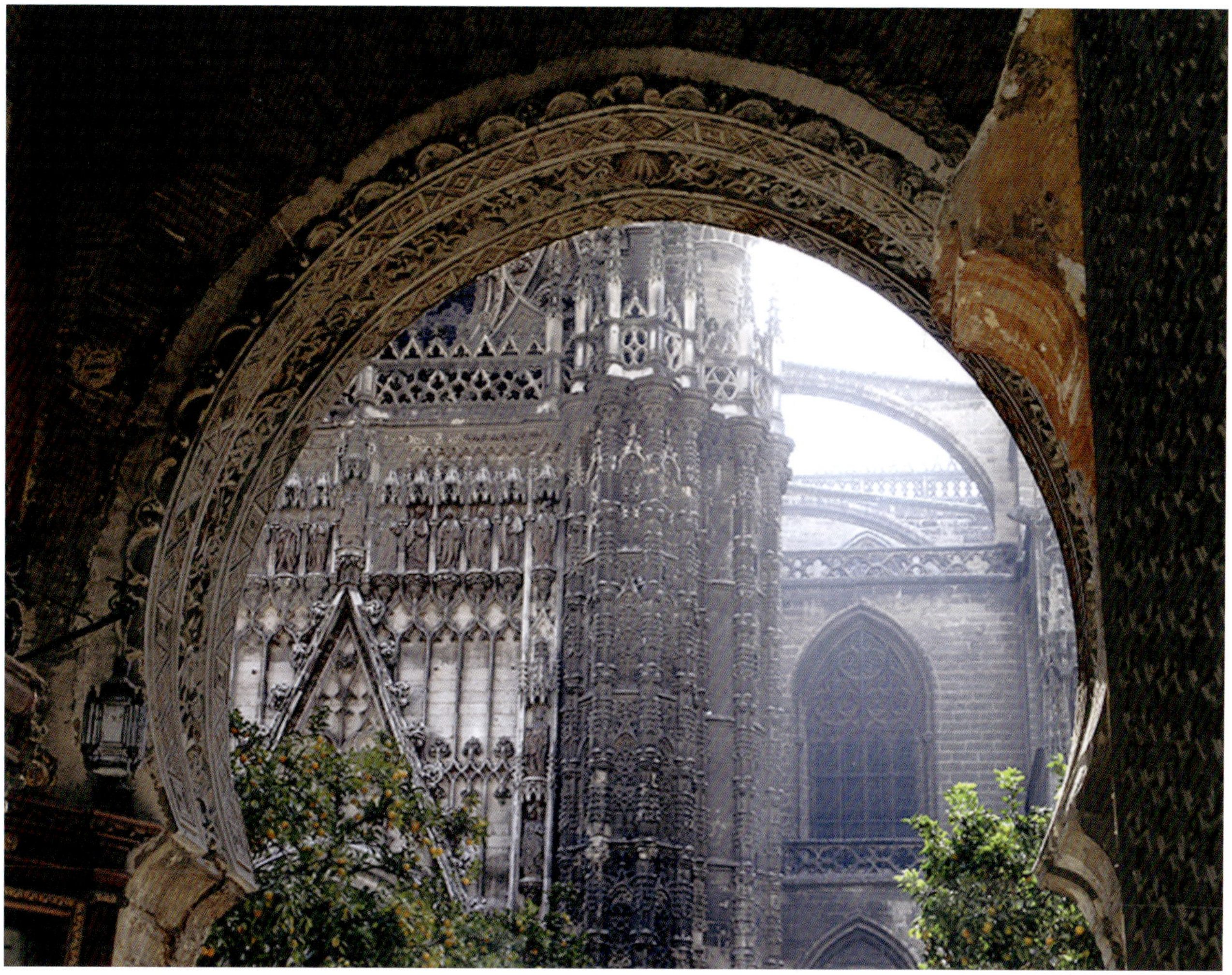

Mezquita Gate, Sevilla 2004–5, Photograph, 8 x 10 inches

93

CHRONOLOGY

INDIVIDUAL EXHIBITIONS

2007 Espace Kaleo, Rochefort-en-Terre, France

2006 Santa Fe Camera Center, Santa Fe, NM

2004 Galleria Can Serrat, El Bruc, Barcelona, Spain

2003 Espace Loisirs, Vallauris, France

1999-00 Harwood Museum, Taos, NM
(Collaborative Installation with Ford Robbins)
(Curator: David Witt)

1998 St. John's College Gallery, Santa Fe, NM

1997 Dankook Cultural Center, Ashland, OR

1985 Retrospective Exhibition
Galeria Jaime Torres Bodet, Gallery of the City of Guadalajara, Mexico

1984 Retrospective Exhibition, Museum of Technology, Mexico City, Mexico

1980 Gallery Amerasia, Washington, DC

1979 "Two Dimensions," Council of the Arts, The Miller's House, Fairfax, VA

1976 Mikimoto Gallery, Tokyo, Japan

1975 Gallery of the American Club, Tokyo, Japan

1975 American Cultural Center, Tokyo, Japan

1974 Galerie Kan, Kyoto, Japan

1973 Gallery of the Mitsui Bank, Kobe, Japan

GROUP EXHIBITIONS

2007 Musee, Chateau Rochefort, Rochefort-en-Terre, France

2004 Espace Grand Jean, Vallauris, France

2003 Galerie Aqui Siam Ben, Vallauris, France

2000 Segreto Contemporary Art, Santa Fe, NM

1999 Cline LewAllen Gallery, Santa Fe, NM
(FOCA Artists; Curator: Helen Heninger)

1990-91 Art of Japan Gallery, Santa Fe, NM

1987 Pyramid Atlantic, Washington, DC
(Curators: Helen C. Frederick, Lillian Fitzgerald)

1986 Sculpture Today, Old State House, Hartford, CT
(Curator: Rebecca Matlock)

1986 Gallery K, Washington, DC

1985 Galería Orbe, Cancún, Mexico

1984-85 Galería Mer-Kup, Mexico City

1985 "The Artist and the Amate", Galería de la Banca, Mexico City (Sponsored by the Secretary of the Treasury, Mexico. Curators: Javier Martinez, Ramon López Quiroga)

1984-85 "The Artist and the Amate", Museum of Monterrey, Monterrey, Mexico (Curators: Javier Martinez, Ramon López Quiroga)

1984-85 Galería López Quiroga, Mexico City

1984-85 Prints D'Goya, Mexico City

1984-85 Kalistea Gallery, Mexico City

1984 Screens at the Kin, Mexico City
(Works by invitation)

1984 International Corn Products, Executive Salon, Latin American Headquarters, Mexico City, (Curator: Graciela Kartofel)

1981 Northern Virginia Regional Art Show, Annandale, VA (Juried exhibition)

1980 Council of the Arts, Members Show, Fairfax, VA
(Judge: Hank Harmon)

1978 Art League of Washington, DC, Annual Members Show (Judge: Jack Perlmutter)

1976 National Association of University Women, XXII Annual Print Exposition Invitational, Tokyo

1976 Four Printmakers, Galerie 412, Tokyo

1973 Sei Boku Kai (Pure Ink Group), Luna Hall, Ashiya, Japan (Works by invitation)

GRANTS AND AWARDS

2007 Morbihan, France, Government, Rochefort-en-Terre (artist residency administered by Maryland Institute College of Art)

2006 Wellspring House, Ashfield, MA (artist residency)

2004 Can Serrat, Barcelona, Spain (artist residency)

2003 Air Vallauris, Vallauris, France (artist residency)

2000 Anderson Center for Interdisciplinary Studies, Red Wing, MN (artist residency)

1988 Cam Memorial Lecture, New York Public Library

1987-88 New York Public Library, Allen Room (space and assistance for research and writing)

1987 International Cultural Society (grant for research and travel)

1985-86 Library of Congress, Asian Division (space and scholarly assistance)

SELECTED LECTURES AND PRESENTATIONS

2007 Southwest Literary Center, Santa Fe, NM, reading from *Looking Around*,

1988 New York Public Library, Cam Memorial Lecture, New York, NY

1988 University of Pennsylvania, Pre-Columbian Society, Philadelphia

1987 New York Public Library, Rare Book Room, consultation, Korean books

1987 Dard Hunter Museum, Papermaking Conference, Appleton, WI

1986 Folger Library, Washington, DC

1986 Smithsonian Institution, Freer Gallery, Washington, DC (for Smithsonian and Freer staff)

1986 Library of Congress, consultation and staff workshop on Mexican pre-Columbian paper

1986 Commentary for KBS-TV, *5000 Years of Korean Art*, Asian Art Museum of San Francisco

1985 Commentary for Canal 11, *Caligraphía*, Instituto Nacional de Bellas Artes, Mexico City

EDUCATION

1963 AB Hunter College, New York (cum laude, Phi Beta Kappa, Regents Scholar)

1963-64 Graduate Studies: Johns Hopkins University, Baltimore (University Scholar, C.L. Pack Fellow)

1987 Graduate Studies: University of Pennsylvania, Philadelphia

1975-76 Lithography with Gaston Petit, Atelier Petit, Tokyo, Japan

1973-75 Calligraphy with Tanino Shigeko, calligrapher, Osaka, Japan

1969-70 Chinese landscape painting with Park Se Won, chair, Department of Fine Arts, Seoul National University

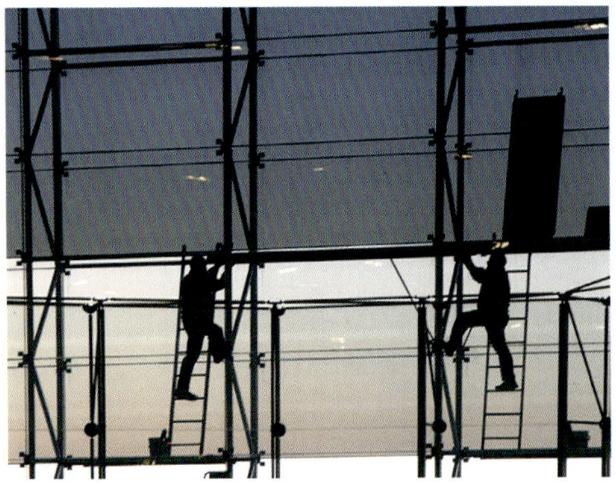

Zurich Windows 2006, Photograph, 8 x 10 inches

INDEX OF TITLES